JOY

Other books by Céleste perrino Walker:

Adventist Family Traditions (Pacific Press)
Eleventh Hour (Pacific Press)
Guardians (Pacific Press)
I Call Him Abba
Making Holidays Special (Pacific Press)
Making Sabbath Special (Pacific Press)
Midnight Hour (Pacific Press)
More Power to Ya!
Prayer Warriors (Pacific Press)
Prayer Warriors: The Final Chapter (Pacific Press)
Sunny Side Up

To order, **call 1-800-765-6955.**

Visit us at www.reviewandherald.com for information on other Review and Herald® products.

JOY

THE SECRET OF BEING CONTENT

CÉLESTE PERRINO WALKER

REVIEW AND HERALD® PUBLISHING ASSOCIATION
HAGERSTOWN, MD 21740

This book was
Edited by Gerald Wheeler
Copyedited by Delma Miller and James Cavil
Cover designed by FreshCut Design
Interior designed by Candy Harvey
Electronic makeup by Shirley M. Bolivar
Cover photo by Nalle Goelbasl/Getty Images/Taxi
Typeset: 11/13 Bembo

PRINTED IN U.S.A.

09 08 07 06 05   5 4 3 2 1

R&H Cataloging Service
Walker, Céleste perrino, 1965-
    Joy—The secret of being content.

    1. Joy and sorrow.   I. Title.

        152.42

ISBN 0-8280-1809-X

"But let all those rejoice who put their trust in You;

let them ever shout for joy,

because You defend them;

Let those also who love Your name

be joyful in You."

—*Psalm 5:11, NKJV*

For Joanne, who walks in JOY and inspires me.

CONTENTS

CHAPTER 1

WHAT IS JOY?

THERE ARE PRAYERS, AND THEN THERE ARE *PRAYERS*. "Please, Lord, help me be on time for my meeting" is not of the same caliber as "Lord, show me how You make a difference in my life." I think that while any serious Christian is going to mutter an awful lot of the first, one day he or she will scream the second—and when that happens, *look out!* Things will never be the same again.

I distinctly remember that day in my life. Faith without works may be dead, but works without faith is very tiring, and I was extremely tired. I did all the right things. I said all the right things. I accepted all the right positions. I prayed all the right prayers. I read all the right books. But I was bone-tired of living and being disappointed. I was exhausted from the endless trying and failing. Because even when your life seems like a success on the outside it can be the most intimate failure to you personally.

Circumstances beyond our control may make it nearly impossible for us to do what is right. Take Moses, for instance. I understand exactly his predicament when he stood by that rock. "Moses and Aaron went from the assembly to the entrance to the Tent of Meeting and fell facedown, and the glory of the

Lord appeared to them. The Lord said to Moses, 'Take the staff, and you and your brother Aaron gather the assembly together. Speak to that rock before their eyes and it will pour out its water. You will bring water out of the rock for the community so they and their livestock can drink.'

"So Moses took the staff from the Lord's presence, just as he commanded him. He and Aaron gathered the assembly together in front of the rock and Moses said to them, 'Listen, you rebels, must we bring you water out of this rock?' Then Moses raised his arm and struck the rock twice with his staff. Water gushed out, and the community and their livestock drank" (Num. 20:6-11).

As his staff cleaved the air in two and he gave the rock a re-sounding thwack he was probably thinking, *These people are driving me crazy. It doesn't matter how much I do for them—they don't appreciate it. No matter what I say, they don't listen. I forfeited my career in shepherding (in which I had a peaceful life) to drag them out of slavery. Do I even get a thank-you for my pains? No. Obstinate, rebellious . . . if I say it's black, they protest it's white. Or if I say stop, they say go. I've had enough!*

And with one hasty thwack his whole life changed. Was Moses a bad man? No. Was he walking with God? Yes. He had been journeying with God before that moment, and he would continue to do so afterward. He just took a significant detour. And even in his detour, God was there despite the fact that he ignored Him. So how could he, in the blink of an eye, say adios to God and go his own way? Why after the struggle of a life-time did he give in to his impulses?

Why? Because Moses was tired. He was worn out from beating his head against the obstinacy of the Israelites. Israel's leader had been saddled with them for life, and try as he might, he couldn't get them to change. Not only that, but they wore him down with their waywardness, their insensitivity, their disregard for him and for God.

I know where Moses was that day because I've been there myself. Instead of a rock, I had just a bank of snow outside the window and tears sliding down my face as I stared out at it. The landscape was bleak, frozen, and barren, just like my soul. Some prayers are requests, and some are heart cries. Mine shattered every illusion in my life. I abandoned any form of prayer I had ever learned and screamed into the stillness of my house, "Where are You? Why don't You do something? Either You show me how believing in You makes a difference in my life or I won't believe in You anymore. If You don't have any power, then why should I do what You want?"

You can't pray a prayer like that and not get an answer. Because He *is* powerful, and He is with us. And when we seek with all our hearts we will find Him. " 'For I know the plans I have for you,' declares the Lord, 'plans to prosper you and not to harm you, plans to give you hope and a future. Then you will call upon me and come and pray to me, and I will listen to you. You will seek me and find me when you seek me with all your heart. I will be found by you,' declares the Lord, 'and will bring you back from captivity. I will gather you from all the nations and places where I have banished you,' declares the Lord, 'and will bring you back to the place from which I carried you into exile'" (Jer. 29:11-14).

In novels God would have shown me some miraculous sign, and I would have fallen on my face to worship Him and thank Him for answering me. But life is not a novel, and mine went from bad to worse. Not only did God not seem close; He felt nonexistent. When you hit the bottom and you're lying flat on your back looking up, you can see some interesting things. Even though God appeared as distant as the North Pole, I can now see His footprints distinctly beside mine the whole way.

Pain may block our view of God, but He never abandons us.

But at the time I couldn't see it because I took my eyes off God, just as Moses did. As I looked at what was around me I saw all the things wrong with my life. All the circumstances that I could not tolerate for another second. Both Moses and I made a choice and let the things around us determine our destiny. In effect we said, "Here you go, Satan. We give up. Since you're the most powerful, you take over."

Not until years later did I finally figure out what went wrong that day and why. Somewhere between the baptismal stream and that snowy day I had lost my joy. Joy is a gift God gives us. But He doesn't offer it to us as a reward for finally becoming a good enough Christian. Rather, joy is the emotional fuel for the journey—and He provides us with a spare tank for the long haul.

We can't wait for life on earth to get good before we have joy. I'm sorry to be the bearer of bad tidings, but things ain't gonna get any better than this. In fact, they'll probably become a whole lot worse. Jesus said to the Father, "I am coming to you now, but I say these things while I am still in the world, so that they may have the full measure of my joy within them. I have given them your word and the world has hated them, for they are not of the world any more than I am of the world. My prayer is not that you take them out of the world but that you protect them from the evil one" (John 17:13–15).

"The world has hated them," Jesus observed of His disciples. But He's also talking about us. The world also hates us. Don't expect a pat on the shoulder from it. Look for a cold shoulder. But what the world gives us isn't important. We can still have a full measure of joy in us. Joy is not the giddy emotion of happiness that changes depending on how the weather is like outside or what we ate for breakfast or how much we have to pay in taxes. Rather, joy is constant and abiding.

If Moses had had joy that day beside the rock, he would have blocked out the Israelites and their whining and concentrated instead on the big picture. He would have realized that it was God's way or no way, and he would have acted accordingly. Instead, he let circumstances overwhelm him.

What's going on in our lives can seem impossible to ignore. After all, joy is not some kind of immunization against sin or a happy pill that makes us oblivious to reality. But when we have it inside us, when we are using it as Jesus intended, it will give us a perspective that we can't otherwise have. Joy takes us out of the present and focuses our mind on the future. It keeps our mind-set steadfastly where it ought to be—on God's divine plan.

Let me give you an illustration. A group of people are stranded on an island. One day a ship comes by and rescues all but two men. The vessel does not have enough room to take everyone, but the captain promises that he will return for the two remaining castaways. Days turn into weeks, and weeks become months. The two men fight to survive from one day to the next.

A pack of wild dogs lives on the island and competes with the men for the available food, threatening their lives constantly. They have to travel through a treacherous path down a steep, rocky slope to reach their only source of potable water. Venomous snakes make any venture beyond their shabby little hut dangerous. Poisonous jellyfish sun themselves in the shallow waters by the shore of the island, so the castaways cannot even swim without fear. Still, they struggle on, relying on the captain to keep his word.

One day the first man, tired of waiting, decides that the captain is not coming back after all. He builds himself a small raft. When the second man refuses to join him, he strikes out alone.

Unfortunately, about a mile from shore his raft capsizes and he drowns before he can swim back to the island.

The remaining man continues to fight for survival every day. Constantly he reminds himself of all the things he will do when he reaches civilization again. Thinking about all of the people that he will be reunited with when he goes home, he is grateful for every new day of life, because he is one day closer to going home and leaving the island for good.

The day finally arrives when the captain returns to pick up the man. Everything is even better than he imagined it would be. Tiny, minuscule details—the things he would not have even noticed before—are now important to him. Everything matters, because now he realizes what it's all worth.

His emotional tank was full of joy. He endured through his time on the island because of the captain's promise to return and take him to a better life. Some days he was not happy. Other days he struggled with discouragement. But he never gave up, because his joy was firmly anchored in the captain's promise. *For the joy of returning home he endured life on the island.*

If we do not have joy in us, then life is nothing more than an exercise in futility. In the same way, Jesus' death on the cross could have been a similar exercise in futility if He was not securing eternal life for us.

"Let us fix our eyes on Jesus, the author and perfecter of our faith, who for the joy set before him endured the cross, scorning its shame, and sat down at the right hand of the throne of God. Consider him who endured such opposition from sinful men, so that you will not grow weary and lose heart" (Heb. 12:2, 3).

The writer of Hebrews tells us to consider Jesus and all that He endured from sinful human beings so that we ourselves will not grow weary of this life and lose heart. For the "joy set before him" He endured the cross. The joy could hardly be the cross itself. So we have to look further ahead at something set before Him, something in the future: our salvation and our eternal life with Him in heaven, at His home.

Reunion is the completion of joy. John spells this out in one of his letters. "I have much to write to you, but I do not want to use paper and ink. Instead, I hope to visit you and talk with you face to face, so that our joy may be complete" (2 John 12). When loved ones are apart from each other, it is joy that bolsters them up during periods of homesickness. They look forward to meeting again. When they do, their joy is complete—it lacks nothing.

Jesus gives us His joy for the same reason—that we, considering the joy set before us (heaven), will not let our lives be ruled by the immediate, by the demanding, by what looks good at the moment. Instead, we are to use His joy to filter out what is temporary and concentrate on what is permanent. In heaven, when we see Jesus, our joy will be complete.

But joy doesn't stop with us. It goes further. Like light, joy can't be confined. Joy touches every aspect of our lives. It affects everyone we come in contact with—including Satan. He hates it. Joy proves, more than anything other than love (and let's face it, if you don't have joy you can't have love, either), that Jesus actually *lives* in our hearts. Lack of joy is the hallmark of Satan.

Joy originated with God. In the beginning there was joy. God is the most joyful being in the universe. How do we know that? Because creation reverberates with joy. God spoke something into existence, and it was good—behold, it was *very good*. After sin, confusion entered creation and darkness covered the earth. I think that's why joy is so important. In the darkness joy shines like a beacon. Like light or beautiful music, it can't be ignored.

The last time I went to the symphony I sat in the balcony, looking down on the orchestra pit. The musicians tuned their instruments. Violins, cellos, violas, basses, flutes, oboes, saxo-phones, and trumpets squeaked and squawked like a flock of disgruntled barnyard chickens. When the sound of the instruments died down, a rustle fluttered through the audience. I caught my breath. The anticipation was agony. It seemed as if entire lifetimes crawled by before the conductor took his position. Then, at his slightest movement, strains of music began to flow from the orchestra.

The music itself seemed alive. It floated above our heads, it pierced our hearts, it wrapped around us like a comforting blanket. Then it pulled us behind it, dragged us up, hurled us down. We were at its mercy. When the music was joyful, we were joyful. As it turned somber, we were somber. And when the music was giddy, we felt giddy.

I like to think of creation as the symphony of joy with God as the conductor. At a single wave of His baton the water and land merged. Fish teemed in the ocean. Animals capered on land. Stars, like diamonds, twinkled in the sky. Plants grew, bursting forth with fruit and grain. And everywhere crescendos of joy.

Joy manifests itself in the types of plants, the different animals, the vibrant colors, the textures, the beauty of what God has accomplished. It carries us away, making us feel delight at the awesome creative burst. No downhearted sad sack could ever have brought our world into being. And what we're seeing is only a pale shadow of what the earth started out as.

Sadly, things here *don't* go as planned. Bad things happen to good people. But guess what? They strike bad people, too. The difference is in how one reacts to them. It shows the world whether a person is full of joy or not.

Horatio Spafford was born in North Troy, New York, on October 20, 1828. As a young man he had established a highly successful law practice in Chicago. Despite his financial success, though, he maintained an active interest in spiritual affairs and was close to D. L. Moody and other evangelical leaders of his era.

Horatio married a woman named Anna, and they had five children, four girls and a boy. The boy died tragically when he was very young. This disaster alone would be enough to stagger most of us, but Horatio and Anna pressed on. A short while later, with the profits from his law practice, Horatio invested heavily in real estate on the shore of Lake Michigan. But, as the story goes, Mrs. O'Leary's cow kicked over a lantern and started the great Chicago fire, and Horatio's land holdings went up in a puff of smoke.

Literally.

Deciding to go to England to join and assist Moody in his campaign there, and feeling that the family needed a break, Horatio booked them all passage on a luxury steamer, the S.S. *Ville de Havre*. But before they could leave, Horatio found himself detained on business. Sending his wife and four little daughters on ahead, he promised that he would join them shortly.

Anna and the girls boarded the *Ville de Havre* and began their voyage. On November 22, in the middle of the Atlantic, the English vessel *Loch Earn* rammed the *Ville de Havre,* and the latter sank in 12 minutes. Of the hundreds on board, only 47 survived, including Anna Spafford, rescued unconscious floating on a spar and taken by rescue ship to France. From Paris she cabled two heartbreaking words to her husband:

"Saved alone."

Horatio left immediately to join his grieving wife. As they traveled back across the Atlantic, he asked the captain to let him know when they passed over the spot where his daughters had drowned. Eventually the captain sent for him, and Horatio stood at the rail looking down on the rolling waves. It was here, on this spot, that Horatio G. Spafford wrote these words:

> "When peace, like a river, attendeth my way,
> When sorrows like sea billows roll—
> Whatever my lot, Thou hast taught me to say,
> It is well, it is well with my soul."

That is the essence of joy. It is what keeps us from curling up and dying when everything—*everything*—in life is going wrong. Jesus gave us two gifts besides salvation while He was on earth. "Peace I leave with you," He said. "My peace I give you. I do not give to you as the world gives. Do not let your hearts be troubled and do not be afraid" (John 14:27). Later He added, "I have told you this so that my joy may be in you and that your joy may be complete" (John 15:11). Peace and joy.

But peace is another whole book. Let's talk about joy.

CHAPTER 2

WHO'S STEALING OUR JOY?

S O IF JESUS LEFT HIS JOY IN US and we don't have it anymore, who's been stealing our joy? If this were a mystery story, I'd be crazy to give away the villain in the second chapter, but I don't think it will surprise anyone to know that Satan is the thief absconding with our joy. But you knew that already, didn't you? A more relevant question is How is he managing to do it?

In the course of an ordinary day you don't see dazed people wandering around actually seeking their joy. What you observe is hurting people who have no idea that their joy has even been stolen. So how did we get to this sorry state of affairs?

Quite simply, the answer is life.

Life gets in the way. We are first too busy and second too tired to realize half of what we are missing. No culture is immune from the problem. In the land of good and plenty we chase our tails, not only for our livelihood but also for social status and to live the "good life." In developing countries and nations at war or suffering from biological or human-caused disasters people work all day just to survive.

"Nothing is easy here," new missionary Amy Whitsett

wrote of the Phuan Project in Thailand. "People work in their mountainside fields literally from sunup to sundown, simply to survive. And there is no social security for old villagers. They literally work until the day they die.

"All of a sudden, the reality of what I was seeing hit me. What a hopeless existence! Live to work, work to live, with no hope of anything better."[1]

Perhaps most of us are not working from sunup to sundown simply to survive, as the Phuan people and many others do, but we're preoccupied and harried nonetheless. We don't have the time or energy to ponder what we are missing, and if we do, the likely answer is a good night's sleep or a vacation.

This, of course, is just the way Satan likes it. He wants us to be so involved with ordinary life that we starve without being hungry and thirst without the slightest indication that anything is wrong. All the while we never realize the very extraordinary life that could be ours if we only claimed it.

This whole sorry business started, of all places, in a garden. You know the story. Adam and Eve, tilling the soil, walking with God—happy, joy-filled, and carefree. Then Satan entered the picture and told them they were missing out. Eve, then Adam, ate the fruit. They're kicked out of Paradise, and suddenly they must coax every bite of food from the ground or lug every mouthful of water from the closest stream, lake, or puddle.

But Adam and Eve had a glimpse of what a life of joy was like. They had lived in complete and utter fulfillment, lacking nothing. But for everyone else the concept of living filled with joy and contentment was a hard sell because they had never known what it was like firsthand. Loved ones died, children went hungry, diseases afflicted people, catastrophes happened, wars began and went on and on and on. When life gets in your face, seeing beyond it is next to impossible.

WHO'S STEALING OUR JOY?

I've been there. Haven't you? A deadline looms; a sick child keeps you up all night; you're fighting a cold; office politics make you a nervous wreck; your boss intimidates you; your spouse is distant; a friend betrays you. No matter what the situation is, we have all been there. Our life—or at least certain aspects of it—becomes all-consuming.

As a result, our prayertime becomes a struggle to keep our mind off our problem and on whatever it is we were supposed to be praying about. It isn't unusual for our spiritual life to take a nosedive altogether. The mental, emotional, and sometimes physical energy it requires simply to move from one day to the next demands all of our resources and concentration.

Moreover, our lack of joy contributes in still other ways toward making us worse off than ever. Dallas Willard explains it well: "Failure to attain a deeply satisfying life always has the effect of making sinful actions seem good. Here lies the strength of temptation. . . . Normally, our success in overcoming temptation will be easier if we are basically happy in our lives. To cut off the joys and pleasures associated with our bodily lives and social existence as 'unspiritual,' then, can actually have the effect of weakening us in our efforts to do what is right."[2]

It's a vicious circle. Our lives are mundane, lived in hardscrabble fashion, gotten through by the skin of our teeth day after day. Because we do not have the deep satisfaction that a life of joy brings, temptation is harder to resist. A life without joy creates a constant search for pleasure to fill the void. Pleasure often leads to excess and sin, driving joy further and further away.

In *The Screwtape Letters* C. S. Lewis writes about a senior demon giving advice to his nephew on how to tempt humans. Uncle Screwtape says: "Never forget that when we are dealing with any pleasure in its healthy and normal and satisfying form, we are, in a sense, on the Enemy's ground. I know we have won many a soul through pleasure. All the same, it is His invention, not ours. He made the pleasures: all our research so far has not enabled us to produce one. All we can do is encourage the humans to take the pleasures which our Enemy has produced, at times, or in ways, or in degrees, which He has forbidden. Hence we always try to work away from the natural condition of any pleasure to that in which it is least natural, least redolent of its Maker, and least pleasurable. An ever-increasing craving for an ever-diminishing pleasure is the formula. It is more certain; and it's better *style*. To get the man's soul and give him *nothing* in return—that is what really gladdens our Father's heart."[3]

Or maybe in your life the shoe is on the other foot. Trials, instead of pushing you from God, actually drive you toward Him. Congratulations! You have taken the first step toward living a joy-filled life. But if you let it stop there, when the pressure lets off you'll swing the other way. Such trials often make it easier to seek God, but in their absence we drift away content without Him because we don't "need" Him as much. The key then, it would seem, is to find that solid middle ground where joy sustains us in both the stress of life and also during its less-tumultuous periods.

Hebrews 11:8-10 holds part of the answer to this dilemma:

"By faith Abraham, when called to go to a place he would later receive as his inheritance, obeyed and went, even though he did not know where he was going. By faith he made his home in the promised land like a stranger in a foreign country; he lived in tents, as did Isaac and Jacob, who were heirs with him of the same promise. *For he was looking forward to the city with foundations, whose architect and builder is God.*"

The patriarch had a vision. He wasn't dwelling in the here and now so much as he was living for the hereafter. Abraham "obeyed and went"; he "made his home . . . like a stranger"; he "lived in tents." Why? Not because he got up one day and decided he wanted to put some challenge into his life. Not because he was trying to make a statement. And not because his morning's Wheaties gave him extra energy. No, he had a vision. He was looking forward.

That same vision drove Abraham, Moses, David, and all the men and women of faith listed in the eleventh chapter of Hebrews. It is what motivated William Miller, Joseph Bates, James and Ellen White, John Loughborough, and all the great Adventist pioneers. God's people all through the ages have seen a better place, a "city with foundations, whose architect and builder is God."

This vision is what *should* compel every Christian. It encourages the Phuan converts, as Whitsett goes on to tell us: "I pictured heaven—streets of gold, mansions made of precious gems, robes of light, soft green grass, no mud, no weeds, no hard work just to survive. Heaven will be the opposite of all that these villagers know. Hallelujah! All of a sudden I saw the baptismal candidates through different eyes. They now have hope for something better. They may still have to live to work and work to live, but they now have the best retirement plan they could ask for."[4]

What are we all in this world but strangers and aliens? Should it truly surprise us that satisfaction, deep contentment, and happiness are so elusive? Not really. We've been sold a bill of goods by marketing experts who insist that we can have it all. Not only that we can, but we should have it all—that we deserve it. So we grow up expecting it. We believe that if we do all the right things—make the right motions, get the right grades, apply to the right schools, get the right jobs—life will be easy.

It's this idea of deserving nice things that I find hard to swallow. I used to have a friend who, anytime something nice happened to me, said that she was happy for me and that I deserved it. When she came over to my house for the first time she looked out the French doors at the view of the Taconic mountain range that lies to the southeast of the house and declared, "This is beautiful. And your house is beautiful. You should be so happy. You deserve it."

The woman lived in a shabby apartment not far from a major thoroughfare. Was I then to assume that unlike me she didn't deserve to live in a new house with a beautiful view? And what about the family whose house burns down? Do they deserve that? And the husband who is laid off? And the elderly person who slips on the icy staircase, falls, and breaks a hip? I'm afraid if we all got what we deserved, our world would be an even sorrier place for all of us.

No, we don't get what we deserve—and a fortunate thing it is, too. In the scheme of things how good we are doesn't count a bit. I could do virtuous deeds from now until the day I dropped dead, but it wouldn't help me. Because the Bible tells us that we deserve death forever. "For the wages of sin is death, but the gift of God is eternal life in Christ Jesus our Lord" (Rom. 6:23, NKJV).

The reason we feel like strangers here is not that we look different from others, or even that we always act different from others (though hopefully we do). It's sad to say, but there are times non-Christians act more Christlike than some professed Christians do. No, the reason we will always be strangers here is that we have chosen Jesus, and anyone who hasn't sides with Satan. That makes us like fish out of water.

A fish out of water flops around and gasps. It will dry up. And, unable to breathe atmospheric oxygen, it will die. Like fish out of water, we are living in the wrong environment. We're immersed in the pollution of sin. Without God's Spirit in our lives we won't be able to live where we've been transplanted. And without God's joy in our hearts we might somehow survive, but we can't flourish.

Yet each day millions of us make our way painfully through life, gasping through each breath, dying inch by inch. And the most wonderful news is that we don't need to! We don't have to suffer through another moment. Jesus gave us His peace, His joy. I like this quotation, a favorite of renowned illustrator Tasha Tudor. Fra Giovanni, an old monk, wrote it to his patron. "The gloom of the world is but a shadow; behind it, yet within our reach, is joy. Take joy."[5] Joy, like salvation, is a free gift. What are we waiting for? Let's take joy!

Satan is mistaken if he thinks he can take what is our rightful inheritance. But we must look at life as God means for us to see it—in the light of eternity—in order to thwart Satan's attempts to steal joy from us. After all, he will do everything possible to convince us that our joy is gone. But we are the only ones who can release its power.

The most common thing people say when they write to me about my books in the Prayer Warriors trilogy is that seeing what is going on in the spiritual dimension changed the way they view things and how they pray. Suddenly they find they are aware of how Satan seeks to manipulate them through circumstances. I had a similar experience that occurred because of this book. Not long ago my husband and I were going through a situation in which so much of our life seemed to be collapsing around us. People who should have been supportive were making things extremely difficult for us.

I found myself thinking, *Even though this situation is so overwhelming and I can't see a way around it, I know it's only temporary.* At that moment a phrase popped into my head: "You intended to harm me, but God intended it for good" (Gen. 50:20). It took me a minute to place who had said it and why. Then I remembered that Joseph had told it to his brothers, who feared that he would hold a grudge against them after their father died. The more I thought about Joseph and his situation, the more I could relate to it.

Think about this kid who became Pharaoh's right-hand man. The pampered mama's boy and daddy's favorite gets sold into slavery by his own brothers, betrayed by people who should have loved him. Joseph's brothers let jealousy rule their behavior, and he ended up in captivity. I doubt he accepted his fate without tears, despair, or even a recrimination or two. The important thing is that *he didn't act on his feelings—he trusted in God.*

Joseph did not enter slavery willingly. He did not even become a slave in his twilight years so that he would not feel cheated. A young man, he found himself a slave in the prime of his life. Servitude stretched before him as far as he could see. Having no reason to believe that he would ever be anything but a slave, he knew that he would have to abandon any dreams or hopes he had for his life. And yet we don't read that he was a sullen, disobedient slave. On the contrary, his service was exemplary.

"Now Joseph had been taken down to Egypt. And Potiphar, an officer of Pharaoh, captain of the guard, an Egyptian, bought him from the Ishmaelites who had taken him down there. The Lord was with Joseph, and he was a successful man; and he was in the house of his master the Egyptian. And his master saw that the Lord was with him and that the Lord made all he did to prosper in his hand. So Joseph found favor in his sight, and served him. Then he made him overseer of his house, and all that he had he put under his authority" (Gen. 39:1-4, NKJV).

By human standards Joseph had every right to rail against his circumstances, to fall into a black depression, to be angry at the world, even to attempt retaliation or revenge if given the opportunity. If that had been his desire, he could easily have accomplished it when Potiphar's wife tried to seduce him. Instead, he said, "There is no one greater in this house than I, nor has he kept back anything from me but you, because you are his wife. How then can I do this great wickedness, and sin against God?" (verse 9, NKJV).

As he faced a life of slavery, how did Joseph keep his joy when we find ourselves so easily tempted to lose ours to life's small inconveniences: a flat tire, an unexpected bill, scorched soup? The key, I think, is that "the Lord was with Joseph." That is the deciding factor. Joseph was not in his circumstance alone. When we abandon joy in the face of difficult times, we abandon God and we walk alone. Joseph never did that. Or if he did, the Bible doesn't record it. Instead, it tells us how Joseph faced not only slavery but worse.

After refusing Potiphar's wife, who fabricated a lie about his intentions, Joseph goes from "no one greater in this house than I" to prison. Surely now, we think, he'll crack. Surely now he'll wallow in self-pity. He'll indulge in a little cussing. Maybe even some nasty remarks to take out his frustration on an innocent bystander. But no, Scripture tells us that even in prison "the Lord was with Joseph and showed him mercy, and He gave him favor in the sight of the keeper of the prison" (verse 21, NKJV). The jailer ends up turning the care of the prisoners over to Joseph. "The keeper of the prison did not look into anything that was under Joseph's authority, because the Lord was with him; and whatever he did, the Lord made it prosper" (verse 23, NKJV).

OK, so now Joseph's doing pretty well in prison. He's in charge of all the prisoners and pretty much has free rein. But it is still confinement. How long can his spirits remain unflagging in such a situation? How long will his joy shine in such a place? Surely he will become discouraged in a week, a month, six months, a year. "Then it came to pass, at the end of two full years, that Pharaoh had a dream" (Gen. 41:1, NKJV). Though he doesn't know it yet, the dream is Joseph's ticket out of prison and into a bigger and better way of life. In fact, he becomes so high up on the chain of command that the only person above him is Pharaoh himself.

I have to believe that Joseph missed his father and brothers during his time in Egypt. Even though he was now BMOC (Big Man of the Country), he seems to be the sensitive type (the Bible calls him a dreamer) who would take such emotional ties to heart. Still, it was an exciting time in its way. Being Pharaoh's right-hand man had many advantages. His new life had to have exceeded in scope and ambition any possible imaginings that Joseph had ever come up with in his wildest dreams. Not only was he more important and powerful than he could ever have become tending sheep; his life's work now involved saving thousands of people, including his own father and brothers.

So on the one hand you have the life it seemed Joseph was destined to lead (slavery) and on the other you have the life God created for him (ruler over Egypt, second only to Pharaoh). Isn't it the same for us? No matter what situation we face, God has something in mind for us that is bigger and better and more exciting than we could possibly dream. Satan sends difficult circumstances toward us for evil, but God turns them into something for our good.

This is pure speculation on my part, but I have to wonder how great a part Joseph's dreams prior to his slavery had in buoying his spirits. His dreams depict the most important people in his life bowing down to him; then he gets sold into slavery. Did he still keep the dreams close to his heart to help him through the long, dark days? Or did he pass them off as fanciful nocturnal imaginings, not worthy of serious consideration? My own opinion is that Joseph believed strongly in his dreams. Somehow he knew that they weren't the product of an overactive imagination. If he had not believed in them, he would have had no reason to imagine later that he could interpret the dreams of the cupbearer or the baker or Pharaoh. I think that Joseph realized that the dreams came from God and thus helped him to keep his eyes on the joy set before him.

As He did for Joseph, God gives each of us glimpses of this joy every day, but we are often too busy, preoccupied, or just plain hardened to life to notice them. I often find myself ignoring such glimpses as I go through a typical day. This is sad for several reasons. God is reaching out just like someone initiating a conversation or offering silent support, and I am too blind to see. Is this what Jesus meant when He said, "For judgment I have come into this world, so that the blind will see and those who see will become blind" (John 9:39)? In addition, I am not receiving the fill-up in my joy tank that God is offering me. It would be comparable to passing gas station after gas station on a long trip and then finally running out of gas. Was gas available? Yes, but if you don't put it in your tank it won't do you any good. In the same way, joy that we do not internalize does not do us any good when the road of life becomes long and tiresome.

There's a lot to be said for taking time to stop and smell the roses. Something that we might consider the smallest, most insignificant detail of each day—such as simply waking up in the morning—is reason to stop and give thanks. Each loved one in our life is a glimpse—just a mere glimpse—of the joy that awaits us in heaven when relationships will reach their God-given potential and none of them will ever be severed by Satan. Although our world is a dark shadow compared to the beauty of Eden's garden, we will still find countless glimpses of joy in nature each day, even if the only part of it we ever see is the sky and the clouds. The sky can show a rainbow of colors, and the cloud patterns are endless.

What is God saying to us through each of these flashes of joy? He's declaring, "I love you. I am thinking about you. I am here for you. Let Me help you. Let Me refresh you. Let Me lead you."

When my children were still toddlers we'd walk down our long driveway. One or the other of them, usually my son, would spy some interesting object. Chubby little fingers would reach out and clutch the object, holding it close and examining it. Then, invariably, the child would offer it to me.

"Mommy, I have a present for you!"

A child offers us a stone, stick, or leaf. Maybe it doesn't look like much to us, but we accept it in the spirit with which it was intended, even if we can't grasp the full significance of the gift.

How much more should we accept each of the gestures of love our Father shows us throughout the day? We don't often grasp their full significance either, but God will show us if we ask. He will make a deposit in our joy bank, and this will sustain us during a time when we perhaps can't so easily "see" God's gestures of love around us.

I imagine Joseph focused on God's gestures of love, and in his situation, especially his time in prison, that would not have been an easy thing. I know that when I am going through tough times it is even harder to notice and appreciate the good things in life. The roses are still as beautiful and smell as sweet. But, through the dark haze of pain, they seem dim and dull. That is when we have to rely on God even more to help us to "hear" and "see" His messages of love. We know that no matter how hard Joseph had it in prison he stayed close to God, because when the baker and the cupbearer had dreams and God showed him the interpretation, Joseph spoke up immediately. Unable to ignore God's promptings, he allowed the Lord to use him even when he probably felt more like wallowing in self-pity.

We can learn many lessons in joy from Joseph's life. His constancy, his firm grasp on hope, his ultimate triumph, and his humility throughout his triumph—these are all lessons for us. And his story reveals something else, something important, that he himself was not even aware of until he could look back on the whole of his life. Even then he would never know some aspects of how his experience fit into the history of God's people. But in Scripture God lets us see how He was working not only in Joseph's life but also in the lives of the Israelites who would come to Egypt in search of food, food that would not have existed if it had not been for God's presence in Joseph, food that kept His people alive.

I think that for me the most important lesson is how Joseph conducted himself throughout his ordeal. He did not use what had happened to him as an excuse to perpetrate more sin, but instead waited on God to deliver him. Though he must have hoped for ultimate deliverance, he did not let that prevent him from doing his utmost at whatever job was at hand. Joseph did not shirk his duty, even though he knew he was a slave through no fault of his own. Grasping the joy of the future, he scorned the inconvenience of the present and performed every act as if it were God Himself he served.

And that is key for us.

The Bible says, "Work hard and cheerfully at whatever you do, as though you were working for the Lord rather than for people" (Col. 3:23, NLT). This doesn't mean "Work as unto the Lord, for then you can feel superior to others." As someone who has spent a lot of time tied to the "stake" I can tell you that serving the Lord is not the same as having a martyr complex, though there are times I dearly wish it did. It's much easier to let feelings of self-righteousness power your work than to find the energy to give it freely. This verse summons us to that higher level of servitude. It calls us to loving service that expects absolutely nothing in the way of a reward.

Think of it this way. Say God asked you to wash the dishes. You'd do them gladly! Why? Because you love Him and you owe Him a debt you'll never be able to pay. Now, suppose your spouse asks you to wash the dishes. You run through a mental tally of how much you've already done that day, compare it in minutest detail with what they've accomplished that day, and you weigh the results. If you've done more than they have, you might still do the dishes, but grudgingly. You'd wash them even more grudgingly if at the same time your spouse was sitting in the living room reading a book, playing with the kids, or doing something else that was more fun than sticking your hands into dirty greasy water. So you do the dishes, but you make a chalk mark in the column of resentment. Over time you accumulate enough resentment, anger, frustration, and other negative emotions that you end up with a full-blown martyr complex.

Now, what would happen if your spouse asked you to do the dishes and you did them *as if* you were washing them for God? Forget about how much your spouse has or hasn't done that day. Forget what your spouse is doing instead of dishes. Simply offer your service to *God*.

For the past six months I have been "flying" with Flylady (www.flylady.net). The acronym FLY stands for finally loving yourself. And while her primary message is how to get a handle on keeping your home clean (she has a system worked out), the success of her system has to do with an overall change in the thinking that got you stuck in a housekeeping rut in the first place, namely, that you are not loving yourself. In addition to this message, Flylady insists that we must stop "keeping score" in housework (and I think it holds true in every area of a relationship). Take out the trash because you want to live in a nice home, not because you want to "show" your husband how martyred you can be doing his job. Sweep the floor because you would like a clean floor for yourself and your spouse, not because you hope to make him or her feel guilty because the spouse didn't do it.

As Flylady points out, many people living in single-parent homes or by themselves have to do *everything*. They do it, and so can we. Ask yourself this: if my husband/wife was diagnosed with cancer tomorrow, how would I feel about doing their chores as well as my own? Chances are you wouldn't think twice. You'd be more worried about appreciating them and loving them while you are still able. So why can't we do that today as well as in a dire situation?

You'd be amazed what this change of attitude will do to your outlook. If it would save your child's life, would you pick up their dirty, stinky socks off the bathroom floor for the third time in one day? Sure you would. I'm not saying that we should shoulder the cleaning burden (or whatever other burdens you have) all alone and let people walk all over us, but rather that it wouldn't hurt to change our attitudes about service to others. We should give it willingly and happily, as if offered to God, who will appreciate it, and not as if offered to human beings, who might not. Then one day we will be able to look back on our lives, as Joseph did, without regrets, but with much satisfaction and joy.

"'If any man serve me,' said Jesus, 'let him follow me; and where I am, there shall also my servant be: if any man serve me, him will my Father honour.' All who have borne with Jesus the cross of sacrifice will be sharers with Him of His glory. It was the joy of Christ in His humiliation and pain that His disciples should be glorified with Him. They are the fruit of His self-sacrifice. The outworking in them of His own character and spirit is His reward, and will be His joy throughout eternity. This joy they share with Him as the fruit of their labor and sacrifice is seen in other hearts and lives. They are workers together with Christ, and the Father will honor them as He honors His Son."[6]

[1] Amy Whitsett, "We're Here," *Adventist Frontiers,* October 2002, p. 5.

[2] John Ortberg, *The Life You've Always Wanted* (Grand Rapids: Zondervan Pub. House, 1997), p. 70.

[3] C. S. Lewis, *The Screwtape Letters* (New York: Macmillan Co., 1957), pp. 49, 50

[4] Whitsett, p. 5.

[5] In Tasha Tudor and Richard Brown, *The Private World of Tasha Tudor* (Boston: Little, Brown, and Company, 1992), p. 60.

[6] Ellen G. White, *The Desire of Ages* (Mountain View, Calif.: Pacific Press Pub. Assn., 1898), p. 624.

CHAPTER 3

THE SECRET OF BEING CONTENT

AS I WAS TALKING WITH A FRIEND recently while we happened to be in the throes of winter up here in the north country, something he said bothered me a great deal. When I claimed to actually enjoy the winter weather he told me that he didn't believe people who said that. In his opinion they were all pining for tropical beaches, and anyone who said otherwise must therefore be in denial.

Then, too, he sometimes hands down his opinions like pronouncements. Sometimes I can't help wondering if the things he continually said were written in a book somewhere that I hadn't yet read, and I was just ignorant of the facts. For weeks, as I mulled this over, I felt like Nigella Lawson, the British restaurant critic/food writer, who wrote that all the time she was growing up she helped her mother make mayonnaise and didn't think it was the least bit difficult until someone questioned her easy way with it and asked how she kept it from curdling. From then on, she said, she could hardly make a mayonnaise that didn't break. The person had undermined her confidence, a condition that makes the easiest things hard and their enjoyment impossible.

JOY

Did I only *think* I enjoyed the winter because I didn't know any better?

Fortunately, common sense came to my rescue. Living near a major ski area, I know for a fact that many people follow the season around the world, skiing here during our winter and then flying to Australia (whose seasons are opposite ours) to experience their winter, and on and on. I've met such individuals. If they didn't like what they were doing and preferred a tropical beach, they would have been there instead. And where would the Winter Olympics be if people didn't truly enjoy cold weather? Or why would we have winter sports at all, for that matter? If they did not truly enjoy winter, children who are sledding would be wailing rather than shrieking with delight.

I'm not sure where my friend comes by his prejudice, but I know one thing for certain. If he doesn't lose it, *he* will never enjoy the winter and will be pining for tropical beaches while he endures it. Recently I read a book based on the life of Anne Hobbs Purdy, who as a young woman made her way to Alaska to teach in a remote area. In it she questions a native Alaskan about when she'll stop being a cheechako, a greenhorn, and start being an Alaskan. He tells her that some people never become Alaskans. They never learn to like the country the way it is. Instead they just tolerate it.

Here, I believe, is the key to living a more joyful Christian life.

The apostle Paul declared, "I have learned in whatever state I am, to be content: I know how to be abased, and I know how to abound. Everywhere and in all things I have learned both to be full and to be hungry, both to abound and to suffer need. I can do all things through Christ who strengthens me" (Phil. 4:11-13, NKJV). Sitting in prison, cold, hungry, alone, Paul did not wish himself away to a tropical beach surrounded by friends, drinking coconut milk, and feasting on mangoes. He lived where he was, not dreaming of being somewhere he wasn't. It was in the living, in the being cold, hungry, and alone, that he was warm, fed, and comforted by God, who is with us most closely in the terrible ordeals through which we must sometimes pass.

We are used to a life of ease. If, we ask ourselves, it's painful, a drudgery, or difficult, why do it? Can it can be fixed? Then fix it. And if it can be improved upon, we make it better. We don't settle for the status quo, and we don't simply get by— we get ahead. As a result we shirk from any kind of discomfort at all—a point driven home to me at a historical reenactment I attended late one October.

The event was at White Plains, New York. It was the big Revolutionary War event of the season. Usually I portray a French woman, but this time I was an American spy camped with the British. More than 1,500 reenactors had gathered there, making the camps impressive, to say the least.

Now, for the uninitiated, let me pause to explain. Every year hundreds (sometimes thousands) of men, women, and children step back into the eighteenth century (and other time periods) and set up military camps usually at or near the scene of famous battles or forts. I happen to live in the heart of both French and Indian War territory, an event that occurred in the mid-1700s, as well as Revolutionary War territory. To as great an extent as we possibly can, as living historians we re-create the eighteenth century. That means we dress in eighteenth-century clothes, we eat eighteenth-century food, we sleep in military tents, and we interpret for visitors what life was like in the eighteenth century. To anyone who loves history it's fascinating.

Reenactors have a die-hard reputation. Before I became one myself I visited Fort Ticonderoga for a few summers for the French and Indian War reenactment to conduct research on some books I am writing. The first time I went it was threatening rain when we woke up and I fretted that they would call the whole thing off, so I telephoned the ferry we had to take to get to the fort.

"Is the ferry still running?" I asked the man who answered.

"Yup."

"Do you think they'll cancel the reenactment at the fort if it rains?"

A chuckle. "Nope. They don't stop for nothing. 'Bout the only thing that disappoints those folks is that they can't use real bullets."

Which, I found out, is pretty close to the truth. Not that they want to kill each other, you understand. It's just more historically accurate. While most reenactments occur during the summer season, a few take place during the fall and even the winter. This particular event was in October, and we had snow early that year. It didn't stick, but it didn't get too warm, either.

That late in the year temperatures plummeted to the 30s at night and didn't rise much above that during the day. I was sick with a cold but decided to go anyway, because I had looked forward to the event. In addition, I was in charge of cooking food for my unit, so people were counting on me.

That first night, lying on the ground under myriads of blankets, feverish and bone-achingly cold, I would have traded my right arm to be transported home in the blink of an eye to my nice warm comfortable bed. Simply knowing it was a miserable four- to five-hour drive before I could be in any kind of comfort was nearly unbearable. I was convinced I was going to die there by either freezing to death or catching pneumonia. In reality it had nothing to do with my cold or the temperature. The truth was I'd gotten soft.

Even lying there, I wondered how it had happened. I was

THE SECRET OF BEING CONTENT

the girl who would hike and camp in the rain and never let it bother me. Mosquitoes and black flies? No problem; just out-run them. Hungry? Big deal. Cold? Who cared? Tired? No matter how tired, I was always good for a few more miles or whatever it took. And afterward I looked back on those hard-ships with a fierce pride. Blisters, sunstroke, hypothermia—I could take whatever the trail dished out. Come on; bring it on!

Patrick McManus, who wrote, among other things, *A Fine and Pleasant Misery,* a hysterically funny look at the foibles of the great outdoors that lives up to its title, knows what this is like. In some strange way, it is the hardships you endure and the trouble you have that make the trip memorable. The downpour that practically flooded us out at Fort Ti, the freezing tempera-tures of Basin Harbor, the heat at Fort Number 4—I can look back on all those things and feel pride at having not only sur-vived them but having a splendid time in spite of them—or maybe, even because of them. But I worked up to that gradu-ally, and after having it easy for years, the first discomfort was not pleasant at all.

It's hard to admit that you've gotten soft, but it's an easy condition to get into. It creeps up on you too, a little at a time. And generally you're not even aware you've become soft until you encounter a reality check of some kind. Chances are the hikers who wrote these suggestions and left them on comment cards at trailheads didn't realize they had gotten soft either:

"Trail needs to be reconstructed. Please avoid building trails that go uphill."

"Too many bugs and leeches and spiders and spiderwebs. Please spray the wilderness to rid the area of these pests."

"The coyotes made too much noise last night and kept me awake. Please eradicate these annoying animals."

"Need more signs to keep area pristine."

"The places where trails do not exist are not well marked."

"Too many rocks in the mountains."

We can laugh at such people. "Ha! You're in the great out-doors—what do you expect?" But, when you think about it, how different are we from them? We're on Satan's turf living on a planet so riddled with sin and destruction that it's amazing the whole mess still sticks together. Our comment cards might look like this:

"Need less suggestive billboards to keep area pristine."

"Pornography is infiltrating my e-mail in-box and attacking my Web surfing. Please eradicate these annoying predators."

"Druggies and gangs are destroying my neighborhood. Please remove these annoying pests."

"The places where God abides are poorly marked."

"Family relationships need to be reconstructed. Please avoid placing irritating people in families."

I could go on, but you get the picture. Life here will remain the same as long as it continues. No amount of wishing will make it change. The only hope for any of us is in our coming Savior. In heaven this dark place will be a smudge in our memories. And it's those little glimpses of heaven and our sure hope for it that bring us abiding joy in this life.

Somewhere I came across this quote from Richard Hatch, a *Survivor* television program winner. And while happiness and joy are two different things, I think there's a lot of wisdom in what he says. "Happiness comes from being a little uncomfortable as often as possible so you're always learning and growing."* It isn't in our comfort that we grow—it's through our discomfort.

We miss this vital principle too often because we try to skip over the discomfort part. Whether it's physical discomfort or spiritual discomfort or emotional discomfort. Think about your prayers. Just take a minute and list a few of the ones that make your top 10 most days. Go ahead, I'll wait. Write them down to make it easier:

_____ _____

_____ _____

_____ _____

_____ _____

_____ _____

Now look them over. How many are requests to make something easier for you and how many are requests for God to take you somewhere that will make life harder for you? For example, are you praying for someone you'd rather not have any personal contact with? Why not? Surely you know someone like that. Why aren't you praying for them?

Ah, you say, don't ask me hard questions like that. I know. I agree with you. It's human nature. Shunning difficulties, we want the easy fix, the miracle.

Consider Mary and Martha. When their brother Lazarus became sick, they sent for Jesus. What did they want? For Him to come and heal their brother. They knew He could do it. After all, they had seen Him restore others. Did they believe He would rush to their aid? Of course. After all, they were among His closest friends.

So what happened when Jesus delayed? (Not even stuck in traffic, He procrastinated on purpose.) By the time He arrived, it was too late. Or was it? It was certainly too late to fulfill Mary and Martha's request. You cannot heal someone who is already dead. But that wasn't Jesus' goal either, except that Mary and

Martha didn't know that. Devastated with grief, Martha accused Him, "Lord, if You had been here, my brother would not have died" (John 11:21, NKJV). Mary echoed the accusation when she saw Him, repeating her sister's words.

Now, at this point Lazarus had been dead four days. Mary and Martha had experienced his sickness, his death, and his funeral. He was in the tomb, buried, done, finis. Martha, at least, held a shred of hope, for following her accusation, she said, "But even now I know that whatever You ask of God, God will give You" (verse 22, NKJV). Apparently it wasn't much more than a shred, because when Jesus asked for someone to roll the stone back, she protested, reminding Him that the body would stink by that time.

We all know how Jesus raised Lazarus to life. But the important things to consider here are: (1) God's timetable and (2) Mary and Martha's response.

First, let's look at God's timetable. We know that it was different than Mary and Martha's (and presumably Lazarus'), because they called for Jesus when Lazarus was still sick, expecting Him to arrive while their brother was alive. We can only guess at their thoughts up to and until Lazarus died and in the days following, but we know they grieved. "And many of the Jews had joined the women around Martha and Mary, to comfort them concerning their brother" (verse 19, NKJV). They did not wait around, faces wreathed in smiles, content in whatever happened.

Nor were they reconciled to their circumstances. The accusations of both women when Jesus first arrived prove this. They didn't say, "Lord, we're so glad You're here. Is this Your plan for us, or can we expect a miracle?" Instead they blamed Lazarus' death on Jesus because He didn't arrive when they first called Him. "If You had been here," they said, not "Now that You are here." In their minds it was finished, and they were pinning the blame.

It is such a human response to anything: tragedy, expectation, longing, dread. Oscar Wilde wrote: "This suspense is terrible. I hope it will last." But it is not our typical response at all. We want it to be over as soon as possible. The longer it drags on, the more miserable and distressed we feel.

Why are we so anxious over important impending events? Because in every situation we have an agenda to protect and desire a particular outcome. That is why it is so difficult to pray, "Lord, Thy will be done." We want some control over God's will.

Mary and Martha, and probably Lazarus, wanted to guide the divine will, desiring that Jesus heal Lazarus. They didn't seek for Him to raise their brother from the dead. While they were happy He did, certainly, it was not part of their agenda. It is because Jesus had spoiled their agenda that they blamed Him for Lazarus' death. Although they had done their part, Christ did not show up and heal their brother.

In the same way we often short-circuit God's timetable by "helping" Him along. Rebekah and Jacob did this when they tricked Isaac into giving the blessing to Jacob when it rightfully belonged to Esau. God had told her, "Two nations are in your womb, two peoples shall be separated from your body; one people shall be stronger than the other, and the older shall serve the younger" (Gen. 25:23, NKJV). Rather than wait for God to work things out in His own time, mother and son deceived Isaac.

Sarah took a shortcut around God's timetable too. Rather than wait for the son God had promised her, she gave her maidservant to her husband and claimed her maidservant's son. But the boy wasn't the son of the promise. Sarah still had her own son later on. You might say, "Yeah, but in both cases things worked out as God said they would." And you would be right.

But consider this. Jacob had to flee for his life, only to be himself tricked and used by his father-in-law. His wives battled for him jealously all their lives. He was terrified of his brother and cut off from his family for so long a time that during it his mother died and his father became elderly and infirm.

Sarah spent years being jealous of her maidservant and her maidservant's son. It strained her relationship with her husband. In either case, were God's best intentions worked out in the lives of the people involved? No. Why? Because they did not wait on God's timetable.

Waiting on God is a very Adventist thing to do. Our whole religion (the "Adventist" part) is based on this truth alone. We look forward to the second advent of Christ. And yet we've been waiting a long time and are getting tired. Active waiting takes a lot of energy. It's easy to get distracted by things that seem so much more immediate and pressing.

The early Seventh-day Adventist pioneers weren't cursed with this, because they expected Jesus at any time and they lived like it. But as time went on we as a church became discouraged and grew distracted. When you expect something that continues not to show up, you start to lose faith. Not in the thing itself. We still believe Jesus is coming soon. But our definition of *soon* has begun to shift. It's not within the next five or 10 or 15 years anymore. Now we're wondering if it will be in our lifetime or even our children's lifetime.

God's timetable is unchangeable. He won't modify it because we are waiting. Nor will He alter it because we are discouraged. It's our job to stay on the ball. To keep expecting, to keep watching for what we know is coming. That is a difficult assignment, but one vital to our mission. And understanding this concept goes much deeper than simply renewing our commitment to keep our "Adventism" fresh. We need to truly internalize this truth if we are to reach our full potential for joy. As a people we must not allow Satan to discourage us when things don't happen in the manner or time frame we think they should.

One of Satan's greatest weapons is this very discouragement. If he can demoralize us, then he can make us doubt God, and if we doubt God, where does that leave us? In Satan's back pocket. "For he who doubts is like a wave of the sea driven and tossed by the wind. For let not that man suppose that he will receive anything from the Lord; he is a double-minded man, unstable in all his ways" (James 1:6-8, NKJV).

Our second point to consider is Mary and Martha's response to Jesus' delay and the subsequent frustration of their agenda. We have determined that the two sisters wanted Jesus to heal Lazarus, but that didn't happen, at least not the way they expected it to. The Bible tells us that they spent their time after Lazarus' death grieving and being comforted by their friends. No longer preparing for a miracle or even looking for one anymore, they had the funeral and mourned. When Jesus finally showed up, they blamed Him for taking too long to be of any earthly good.

But Jesus never intended to be of earthly good in the first place. He had in mind eternal good. "Then many of the Jews who had come to Mary, and had seen the things Jesus did, believed in Him" (John 11:45, NKJV). Jesus did not simply (!) raise Lazarus from the dead. He also witnessed to God's mighty and irrepressible power. Mary and Martha were overjoyed when Lazarus was restored to them, but beyond this the miracle saved people for eternity!

Let's suppose that Jesus had simply fulfilled Mary and Martha's expectations. Consider what would have happened if He had hurried to the sickbed of his friend Lazarus, placed His hands on the man's head, and told him to be well. Lazarus would have then leaped to his feet, healed. Now Mary is happy.

Martha is happy. Lazarus is happy. Is anyone saved for eternity who hadn't been before? Nope.

God does not work within our expectations. And why should He? He is God. We cannot put Him in a box. The story of Lazarus is only one of many that illustrate that God works better outside our narrow-minded boxes anyway. We might have our own agendas that color everything that we say, think, do, and expect, but God Himself has an agenda. His is to save people—all people. And if He can do that and adhere to our agenda, it's more a happy coincidence than it is anything we should ever expect.

---

* Richard Hatch, *101 Survival Secrets* (Guilford, Conn.: Lyons Press, 2000).

CHAPTER 4

JOY KILLERS

WHILE SATAN WORKS MIGHTY HARD to steal our joy, at times we simply hand it over to him as if he had every right in the world to it. There's nothing like giving a thief your wallet just because he bumps into you on the street. We abandon our joy by the way we react to life situations. I'll touch on some major ones. I'm sure, if you think about it, you can come up with others as well.

Strife

Satan just loves this one. It wouldn't surprise me to find out that there exist special squadrons of demons whose solitary job is to stir up conflict. Satan invented strife, so maybe that's why it's his particular pet. He started in heaven, pitting angels against each other and then against God. Finally he took his attitude down to earth and incited Adam and Eve to fall out with God too.

You can trace strife from heaven to earth, from Cain's murderous fist to the beast's thirst for blood. It weaves its wicked way through the entire Bible. Human being against God. Human being against human being. The human race against the elements. Relationships are God's most intimate and precious gift, and strife destroys them, so of course it will be one of Satan's most favorite tools. Solomon tells us that "he who loves transgression loves strife, and he who exalts his gate seeks destruction" (Prov. 17:19, NKJV).

Nowhere do we find the effects of strife more obvious than in the marriage relationship. I recently joined a women's Bible study group. Imagine my surprise when the first topic we studied was how to become an excellent wife based on Proverbs 31. *Oh, well,* I thought, *that's all well and good for everyone else, but surely I'm an excellent wife already.* You're familiar with that other proverb about pride going before a fall?

It was with shock and dismay that I discovered wives are to respond to their husbands in love *at all times.* Not just when they're in a good mood. Not just when the children have been angels. Not just when they are feeling well. Not just when their husbands treat them nicely. No, not just in those times. Wives should respond to and treat their husbands in love *even when* the children have been tearing up the house from the moment their little feet hit the floor, *even when* the dishes are not done and the house is a mess, *even when* they are tired and running behind, even when they are catching a cold, *even when* they are under stress, even when their husbands snap at them or treat them unfairly. And this was only one of the things I found out.

Now, ladies, before you get all stirred up, I'm reporting on what I read. For further discussion or illumination, as the case may be, take it up with the author, Martha Peace. The book's title is *An Excellent Wife.* I didn't write it, though after swallowing very, very hard, I do agree with it.

You see, stuff like that is hard to put into practice. Sure, we know it's biblical—that's not really our problem with it. We say "Love your neighbor" and all that, and we believe it. It's just that putting it into practice *in real life* is tough. It's one thing when you are sitting piously in church, your washed and scrubbed little angels lined up like ninepins, your handsome or beautiful spouse beside you, to read "Love your neighbor as yourself" and think, *Oh, sure, I can do that.* But it's quite another to be chasing said angel down the hallway they have just redecorated with permanent markers and love that angel as yourself.

Strife. It's a real problem. Satan knows that any relationship with any other person on the planet has the potential for strife, because when you come right down to it, we are all self-centered. We're all "What's in it for me? What do I get out of it? How can I protect my rights in this relationship?" And God's all "Love your enemies, bless the ones who curse you, do good to those who hate you, and pray for those who spitefully use you and persecute you. Don't resist an evil person. Turn the other cheek. If anyone wants your tunic, give him your cloak, too" (see Matt. 5:39-44, NKJV).

Christianity has always been a paradox. The last shall be first. Lose your life so that you may gain it. But nowhere is this paradox more evident than in our most intimate relationships. The very people who know us best and take advantage of us most are to receive our complete and utter love and service. And we are not to give it grudgingly, but freely and abundantly without reservation, holding nothing back. Furthermore, we are not to expect anything in return. We're not in it for the glory or the praise or even an acknowledgment of our labors. Every act of service, every action of love, is offered as to God Himself. It is for Him, who has given us so much that we cannot even wrap our minds around it, that we do everything.

You can't behave in this way without a deep and abiding joy inside you. Such joy is your anchor, keeping you firmly grounded in the God from whom every good action springs. If you step away from God and do anything of yourself, you have returned to your own self-centeredness. It is possible to do good from the basis of self-centeredness just as much as it is possible to do evil. When you let someone pull out ahead of you into traffic you have done good, right? And if you let them pull out ahead of you so you can take their parking spot or even so you can simply bask in the effects of doing someone something nice, you are still acting from self-centeredness. Only when you are able to let someone whip ahead of you in traffic while they are making rude gestures at you, because God would do it in your place, and give Him the anger and embarrassment you feel as a result, are you acting at His prompting and not your own.

Such an atmosphere makes it impossible for strife to exist. In the age-old debate about submission and authority, which resembles nothing so much as the question about whether the chicken or the egg came first, we can see a tangible example of how this attitude of godly service to others plays out. Wives are to submit to their husbands, but husbands are to love their wives as their own bodies. Which comes first, the wife submitting, or the husband loving? Does it matter? No. They mesh into a godly relationship in which both parties are happy and satisfied.

In the same way, anyone who follows the biblical pattern of treating others in the manner they would like to be treated (regardless of how others deal with them) does not allow strife to exist in their relationships for the simple reason that strife has "I" smack-dab in the middle of it. Remove the "I" out of strife, and you don't even have a word anymore.

And if you take "I" out of the equation, you are left with the question "What is the best and most loving thing for this other person that I'm having trouble with?" Sometimes the best thing—the action that will keep the peace—is to remove yourself from the situation. Joyce Meyers, in her book *Life Without Strife,* says: "We should do everything we possibly can to make a relationship work, and this is especially true in marriage, but the bottom line is this: If a person absolutely does not want to be in a relationship with you, but you keep trying to force it, it will never produce anything but strife. Please remember that strife opens the door for all kinds of other problems."[1]

The Bible offers several examples of people extracting themselves from a situation to prevent strife. Abraham's is one of the most touching. "Then Abram went up from Egypt, he and his wife and all that he had, and Lot with him, to the South. Abram was very rich in livestock, in silver, and in gold. And he went on his journey from the South as far as Bethel, to the place where his tent had been at the beginning, between Bethel and Ai, to the place of the altar which he had made there at first. And there Abram called on the name of the Lord.

"Lot also, who went with Abram, had flocks and herds and tents. Now the land was not able to support them, that they might dwell together, for their possessions were so great that they could not dwell together. And there was strife between the herdsmen of Abram's livestock and the herdsmen of Lot's live-stock. The Canaanites and the Perizzites then dwelt in the land.

"So Abram said to Lot, 'Please let there be no strife between you and me, and between my herdsmen and your herdsmen; for we are brethren. Is not the whole land before you? Please sep-arate from me. If you take the left, then I will go to the right; or, if you go to the right, then I will go to the left'" (Gen. 13:1-9, NKJV).

Abram was so committed to living in peace that he was will-ing to separate from Lot, whom he loved, to avoid strife. Not only was he willing to let Lot go, but he offered him the choice of *his own land*. God had given the land, not to Lot, but to Abram. Unfortunately, rather than return Abram's love, Lot chose what he saw as the best for himself.

"And Lot lifted his eyes and saw all the plain of Jordan, that it was well watered everywhere (before the Lord destroyed Sodom and Gomorrah) like the garden of the Lord, like the land of Egypt as you go toward Zoar. Then Lot chose for himself all the plain of Jordan, and Lot journeyed east. And they separated from each other. Abram dwelt in the land of Canaan, and Lot dwelt in the cities of the plain and pitched his tent even as far as Sodom. But the men of Sodom were exceedingly wicked and sinful against the Lord.

"And the Lord said to Abram, after Lot had separated from him: 'Lift your eyes now and look from the place where you are—northward, southward, eastward, and westward; for all the land which you see I give to you and your descendants forever. And I will make your descendants as the dust of the earth; so that if a man could number the dust of the earth, then your descendants also could be numbered. Arise, walk in the land through its length and its width, for I give it to you.'

"Then Abram moved his tent, and went and dwelt by the terebinth trees of Mamre, which are in Hebron, and built an altar there to the Lord" (verses 10-18, NKJV).

The really interesting thing about this is that while Lot *thought* that the land he had selected was the best, God didn't bless *his* choice. In fact, the "beautiful" land Lot admired harbored the wickedness of Sodom and Gomorrah. Lot chose a rotten apple that appeared good only from a distance. Abram, on the other hand, didn't look to temporal things for his joy. He relied on God, and the Lord blessed him.

David made the decision to separate himself from Saul because his presence was causing strife. "Then David fled from Naioth in Ramah, and went and said to Jonathan, 'What have I done? What is my iniquity, and what is my sin before your father, that he seeks my life?'" (1 Sam. 20:1, NKJV). Jonathan had no answer for the question, but he agreed with David's plan to leave if his father was in fact determined to kill his friend. After laying out his plan to warn David, he said, "But if I say thus to the young man, 'Look, the arrows are beyond you'—go your way, for the Lord has sent you away" (verse 22, NKJV).

Later, after he had given David the signal to leave, he told him, "Go in peace, since we have both sworn in the name of the Lord, saying, 'May the Lord be between you and me, and between your descendants and my descendants, forever'" (verse 42, NKJV). It was important to both Jonathan and David to maintain peace, even if it meant they might never see each other again. David spent years wandering around while Saul hunted him despite the fact that David's rightful place was as king.

Paul and Barnabas parted for entirely different reasons. "Some time later Paul said to Barnabas, 'Let us go back and visit the brothers in all the towns where we preached the word of the Lord and see how they are doing.' Barnabas wanted to take John, also called Mark, with them, but Paul did not think it wise to take him, because he had deserted them in Pamphylia. . . . They had such a sharp disagreement that they parted company. Barnabas took Mark and sailed for Cyprus, but Paul chose Silas and left, commended by the brothers to the grace of the Lord. He went through Syria and Cilicia, strengthening the churches" (Acts 15:36-41).

As you can see, human relationships haven't changed much in the past several thousand years. Since Paul and Barnabas were in a ministry together, it would have been much better if they could have worked their differences out, but either they felt the problem was irreconcilable or they just didn't put in the effort it required. But even then peace was important to them. Jesus said, "Every kingdom divided against itself will be ruined, and every city or household divided against itself will not stand" (Matt.

12:25). Had Paul and Barnabas remained together and not reconciled their differences, their ministry would have suffered.

I could say a lot more about strife, having been caught up in it for the past six years in some family relationships. As a result I can vouch for how it clouds your life and strains your health, how it eats away at your happiness and destroys God's best plans and intentions for you. It's hard to give up in a situation, to let go and let God. But sometimes there is no other solution than to quit striving toward how you think things ought to be and let God make something much more wonderful out of them. Then I can have joy in the present, because I know that ultimately God will work out His purposes, if not here, then certainly in heaven.

Stress

Stress is another major force that drives away joy. The trouble isn't so much the stress itself. It has been around from time immemorial. Even if we didn't work 60-hour weeks and try to be superman or superwoman, we'd still have stress. The old-time farmers who plant their seeds and then sweat out the storms to see if there will be any crop left may work at a slower, more deliberate pace, but they're under stress nonetheless.

Life is a series of stresses. Until they are dead, no one escapes the pressure. That doesn't mean we are helpless against stress, though. We can prevent some forms and control others. Our job, then, is to decide which falls into which category.

A big one for me is the "I can't say no" category. So one of the most important lessons I ever learned was that I was not responsible for doing everything. It wasn't all up to me. I sorted it out in my mind by imagining myself on a train station platform surrounded by stacks of baggage with people milling all around. Suddenly the train whistle blows. People start getting on the train.

Some take their luggage, and some don't. Just because someone doesn't pick up their own suitcases does not mean that it is my duty to do it. Everyone is responsible for their own luggage.

If I try to carry everyone's baggage I may be helping them, but the commandment does not read, "Love your neighbor to the exclusion of yourself." It declares, "Love your neighbor *as yourself.*" There's a very good reason that airlines tell you to put the oxygen mask on your own face before you try to assist someone else. When you are not strong enough to help yourself, you are in no position to aid anyone else. It's hard for us, sometimes, to get our minds around the idea that we should go first, but it is necessary.

Always we should be looking toward the long haul. You may be able to help a lot of people in a short amount of time, but isn't it more important to pace yourself so that you are still around for the end of the race? Pacing yourself will give you other important benefits. You will be better able to notice what is going on around you, thus allowing you to decide whether you are capable of doing something. You no longer just react to a circumstance, but are able to act after careful consideration and prayer. You won't fly off the handle as easily or jump to conclusions as quickly.

In short, your life will be more deliberate. A life lived deliberately will be one that allows you to consult the Holy Spirit more often, and as a result you will hear His voice more frequently. It is a life in which joy in the soul has space to thrive and not get hammered down by outside pressure to perform. The joy in a deliberate life will be unmistakable, like a calm, reflective pool. This is what we should strive for. Pray about the stresses in your life. Ask God to reveal them to you. Then let Him show you how to release them so you can live an increasingly deliberate life.

Disappointment

Most of my childhood—the parts I remember best—took place in the 1970s. Somehow I got the idea that when I grew up, life would turn out all June Cleaverish. Maybe it was because I read books from my parents' childhood and not my own. Or perhaps it was because I was fond of old movies or because I watched a lot of old reruns instead of whatever was popular at the time. I was a very sheltered kid, and it wasn't until much, much later that it began to dawn on me that life was not going to turn out the least bit how I expected.

In my imagined life I would not be a stay-at-home mother who also had to work at a job at home. A home-cooked meal would not consist of Wonder bread and macaroni-and-cheese casseroles. I would serve my family lots of fresh vegetables and vegetable proteins. To do that, I would have to pay attention and learn about nutrition. And I planned to chop fresh vegetables and make nearly every meal from scratch. Furthermore, I would not ship my children off to school at the first opportunity. I was going to teach them myself.

But it didn't work out that way. And before long the refrain that often raced through my brain was "It's not *fair!*"

And you know what? Nothing in life is fair. No, it's not fair that after cleaning and teaching and working and exercising and running errands and paying bills and picking up after kids and dogs I should have to pull the vegetables out of the fridge and start making a supper that takes at least an hour to prepare. No, that's certainly not fair. And it's even less fair that after making and eating supper I will have to clean up and then work some more. But that's nothing compared to what some people have to live with.

During a recent interview the kindly-meaning host asked me, "So you write, you speak, you home-school, you're a stay-at-home mom . . . what else do you do?" The question left me at a complete loss. For a moment I felt entirely inadequate. What else *did* I do? Surely that wasn't it? As I drove home later it dawned on me—surely all that was *enough!*

The reason I felt inadequate is one that drives us all. Surely, we say, as we fly from appointment to commitment, this isn't it, is it? There must be more to life. Because no matter how much we pack into our overloaded schedules, no matter how much we massage our wheezing Filofaxs or Dayrunners or PDAs, all this hectic running around is not going to fill the empty void inside us.

Joy does not come in the haste. Nor does it flourish in it. It's like adrenaline that will surge and surge to meet a crisis, but if the emergency never ends, the adrenaline runs out. Joy can survive amid haste—it can sustain you—but eventually, if you get no respite from the pressure, joy will flicker and die.

Haste causes stress, and together the two work to destroy the joy in any soul. We need to realize that it isn't *more* that we're after, it's less—another of the Christian paradoxes. The less you have, the less you do, and the more content you will be because you'll be able to enjoy it to a much greater degree.

Immediacy

This is the kind of syndrome kids often have, though they're by no means the only ones. It's the "I want what I want when I want it and I want it now" idea, otherwise known as immediate gratification. Not only is it a contagious concept; it's also a highly aggressive one. Once you've experienced immediate gratification a few times, it becomes hard to accept anything less. In fact, the circumstances that force us to delay gratification are often the ones that make us the most miserable and the ones we fight the hardest against.

One of the problems with immediate gratification—and

there are many—is that it erodes self-control. Two ways our society has encouraged immediate gratification are through the increase of retail outlets (now you don't have to wait long enough for someone to make you something or for you to make it yourself; you can buy it already made) and through the use of credit (you don't need to have the money to purchase something—you simply have to agree to pay for it over the course of time). Everything is getting faster. Appliances, technology, and transportation are only some of the ways we are becoming accustomed to having our needs met instantly.

Anything that grants us immediate gratification denies us the opportunity to feel truly grateful, and gratitude is one of the things that contributes to and feeds joy. During a time when I was deeply depressed (something I'll discuss later) I began keeping a "gratitude journal." Every night before I went to bed I listed in my journal five things that I was grateful for. Sometimes it was an easy exercise, but other times I had to struggle to find even five things that I could appreciate.

Besides the obvious benefit of training my mind to look at the positives in my life, knowing that I would be facing that blank page later gave my mind the "assignment" to look for things throughout the day that I could include. In this way I was consciously seeking out positive aspects of my life so that I could later record them. In essence you are training your mind to search for the positives, and many of the unpleasant things will then go unnoticed because your brain does not assign them any importance. They are not significant, because you are not writing them down.

If you want proof of how this works, just decide that you are going to notice a particular type of car. A woman I know recently bought a PT Cruiser. I had never seen one before, though by the time she bought hers they had been out for a few years. Toying with the idea of buying one when it comes time to replace my car, I began consciously looking for them. Suddenly I saw PT Cruisers *everywhere*. I couldn't leave my house without noticing at least a half dozen. Before a week was out I think I'd seen just about every color PT Cruisers come in. Jesus said, "Seek and you will find." We can apply this principle to many areas, including joy.

Besides looking for things to be grateful for, another way to combat immediate gratification is to program delayed gratification into your life occasionally. Rather than making a mail-order purchase by credit card, fill out the order form and send a check. Take the time to write and mail a letter sometimes, instead of sending e-mail. Make something you are capable of, or ask someone else to prepare it for you, and then enjoy the anticipation you feel as you wait for it to be finished. Stand in the longest line at the grocery store. Wait 24 hours before buying something you'd otherwise get on impulse.

Broken Relationships

If you had to break life down and distill it into its most basic and simple concept, you'd have to acknowledge that its nuts and bolts consist of our relationships with others. No person is an island, so they say. We are each responsible to some people and dependent on others. To some extent we are involved with everyone who daily crosses our path. Because such relationships glue life together, it stands to reason that when they are broken, either on purpose or inadvertently, the resulting tension affects our joy.

You will find a lot of issues involved here, probably as varied as the number of broken relationships themselves. Two major factors are anger and lack of boundaries. Many of us (and I include myself here) don't have the kind of coping skills we need when problems come up in a relationship. Sometimes that causes us to bury our anger. Buried anger leads to all sorts of problems and illnesses. It can make us physically sick. In addition, buried anger squelches joy.

Another relationship problem results from a lack of boundaries. One type happens when we want to please others. The trouble is that we do it at the expense of ourselves. If you've ever consented to do something that you really didn't want to do, you have allowed someone to cross one of your boundaries. To protect ourselves, we should have boundaries in place in all areas of our lives: spiritually, physically, and emotionally. You may want to pray about what boundaries are appropriate for you. God knows what they are, and He will tell you.

Some broken relationships will heal, but others never will. All of them will emotionally drain us no matter what the outcome. If you are dealing with a broken relationship, the best thing you can do is to ask God to show you what your part of it is. As you do so, concentrate on the joy in your life to be sure you have the strength to get through whatever might come. Broken relationships are often long-term, ongoing difficulties, and it can be easy to run out of joy before they reach a resolution, if they ever do.

As you can see, we can surrender our own joy in many ways. We must be on guard against it happening. Our joy is a precious gift from Jesus, and we should prize it as such. Although we can live without joy, why would we want to?

If you were the child of the richest person in the world, would you be content living with just a handful of pennies in your pocket? God is our Father. We are His children. Ask for and spend your inheritance.

"Why should not our joy be full—full, lacking nothing? We have the assurance that Jesus is our Savior, and that we may freely partake of the rich provision He has made for us. . . . It is our privilege to seek constantly the joy of His presence. He desires us to be cheerful and to be filled with praise to His name. He wants us to carry light in our countenances and joy in our hearts."[2]

[1] Joyce Meyers, *Life Without Strife* (Lake Mary, Fla.: Strang Communications Co., 1995), p. 106.

[2] Ellen G. White, *That I May Know Him* (Washington, D.C.: Review and Herald Pub. Assn., 1964), p. 142.

CHAPTER 5

JOY VERSUS HAPPINESS

HAPPINESS IS NOT JOY. Talking yourself into thinking that nothing is wrong is not joy—it's denial. Joy is deeper and is like faith. Faith is hoping in something you can't see, believing in the promise of something you can't touch. As a result, joy is looking at the bigger picture and believing in the promise of heaven.

Happiness looks at the prospect of standing in the rain to wait for the bus and declares, "I'm outta here." But joy faces the same thing and concludes, "Any inconvenience in this life is temporary. Something much better is coming."

We could compare joy to peppermint. I have some wonderful mint plants growing in my flower garden. They have soft, light-green fuzzy leaves. Soon they will have beautiful purple/blue flowers. Otherwise they are unremarkable in appearance. At first glance it might seem that there is nothing special about them at all. But crush the leaves and place them in boiling water, and they make the most refreshing tea that you could imagine.

Just looking at the plant doesn't free the flavor. It takes boiling water to release it. Joy lurks inside us, but it doesn't reveal itself until it gets into boiling water. That's when you can taste true joy.

Joy is also like the scent of the flower released by the heel that crushes it. It's not giddiness or what we frequently call happiness. Nor is it that grating yellow smiley face urging you to "don't worry, be happy" all the time. The reality of joy is rooted much deeper than that.

I know people who seem to believe that they are happy if they just plaster on a smile and pretend that everything is wonderful, that life couldn't be any better, even when everything is not wonderful, when they do not feel wonderful, and when their life *could* be better. Such individuals may trick others into believing they are happy, but who benefits?

Happiness dissolves in the face of hardship. That's the difference between happiness and joy. Joy endures through hardship. Happiness is a feeling, while joy is a state of being.

Look at it this way: Life is a series of choices. Every day confronts you with opportunities or obstacles. Your choice is to assign each event its designation: opportunity or obstacle. The events remain the same. Only your designation is important. Which you choose determines many other factors, but one of them is your joy.

It's the old "Is the glass half empty or half full?" scenario. Which is it going to be? If it is half full, your thirst will be quenched. But if it is half empty, your thirst will not be satisfied. It has nothing to do with the water in the glass—only your reaction to it. How you see it—that is what is important. So what is the water to you? Your choice determines more than your destiny. It defines the nature of your trip itself.

Not long ago I found myself struggling with a deep depression. That I, in the depths of such depression, could see joy in life is something of a miracle in itself. So you can believe me when I say that joy can exist even when you are at the bottom looking up. Such joy won't jump out and grab your attention, but it is there if you look for it.

At a recent visit to my midwife for my annual exam we discussed wholistic ways I could deal with my depression. She explained that people in depression replay negative thought patterns in their minds. As she explained it I could see that it was something I had been doing. I determined to practice consciously changing my thought patterns.

I've had a little experience with this problem before. As a teenager I would repeatedly replay negative aspects of my life, and they made me feel worthless. One day as the familiar scenes began to recycle, I said, "No!" out loud, forcefully. I concentrated really hard on something else, diverting my attention until the memories stopped. Next I repeated this procedure again and again, until finally the mental movies ceased altogether.

I'm sure I prayed for the strength to do all that, but I don't remember the specifics, so I won't fabricate details for you. But as I faced the days of my depression, trying to be free of the emotional fog, my ultimate success depended on God and my faithfulness to prayer. Don't get me wrong, however. I'm not an expert on depression. The only thing I know about it is that it is bad—and then it gets even worse.

I am an expert on joy, though. Not because I am constantly in touch with it, but because I know where to find it. I know it exists and am determined to experience it, depression or no depression.

For instance, have you ever considered how hard we try to avoid painful situations? Human beings are averse to pain of any kind. It's no wonder we have a difficult time learning from God when He sends us trials. At the first hint of pain we frantically look for the exit. But joy and pain go hand in hand. Paul said:

"My brethren, count it all joy when you fall into various trials, knowing that the testing of your faith produces patience. But let patience have its perfect work, that you may be perfect and complete, lacking nothing" (James 1:2-4, NKJV).

The joy is in the trial in the same way that the power is in God's Word. The issue is not simply enduring a trial—gritting our teeth, clamping our eyes shut, and bracing ourselves—but whether we can relax and simply "be" in the trial, asking God what the lesson is. Isn't that what Paul is saying? "The testing of your faith produces patience," meaning that moving through the trial, as opposed to ranting and raving about it, makes us patient. As we are better able to relax and "be" in the trial we acquire clearer vision to recognize and to accept the lesson that the trial can teach us.

Then patience has its perfect work, meaning that eventually we start to look for the good or the lesson in the trial as a first response rather than searching for a way out of it, seeking for someone to blame, or even just bracing ourselves to get through it and get it over. David was even able to say, "Let me hear joy and gladness; let the bones you have crushed rejoice" (Ps. 51:8).

I learned this lesson the hard way not long ago on a trip to Washington, D.C., to speak at a writers' convention. I don't like flying or arriving in a strange place at night. And though I usually manage to find my way around, I don't have much confidence in my navigational skills. All this makes me a tense traveler.

When I arrived at the airport in D.C., it was late at night. I would not have known my way around the District even if it had been blazing sunlight, so I arranged to take a shuttle. I must have walked out of the front of the airport five times searching for the shuttles that security guards assured me were lined up waiting to take on passengers. The later it got (and the more announcements over the intercom warning travelers not to accept rides from unauthorized persons), the more anxious I became.

I'm not sure when it finally occurred to me that maybe I was going out on the *wrong level*. I tried the other exit level out to the street, and there, right in front of me, stood lines of shuttles, including the one I was looking for. After making arrangements to ride one, I settled myself in. I was "lucky" to be riding in the front, since I have a tendency to get carsick.

It was Sabbath, I was tired, and all I wanted was my hotel room and sleep. The other people in the shuttle were complaining about the fact that the driver had the window down slightly for some air. I made a valiant effort to tune their querulous voices out. And then the driver turned on some secular music station that between playing loud obnoxious music aired objectionable advertisements with language I thought had been banned from the airwaves. *O God,* I thought, *please make that radio break. It's Sabbath, and it's hard enough to have any peace with those women in back arguing. This is just too much.*

And I sat there confidently expecting that radio station to crackle and go off the air while the driver zipped around and in front of cars at approximately 300 miles an hour (at night on a highway that had at least 50 lanes). But you know what? The radio station continued to blare until the shuttle finally dropped me off at my hotel room close to midnight, exhausted, my ears ringing.

The only thing that kept going through my head on that torturous ride was *Why, God? You know it's Sabbath. You know I don't want to listen to this garbage. Is it such a small thing to ask that You make it stop? Surely this can't be Your will.*

You see, I was not "being" in the trial. Instead, I was whining in the trial—whining and squirming and trying desperately to get out of it. That's not how you perfect patience. Nor is it how you grow joy.

Relaxing during pain to make it easier is not an unknown

concept. Ask any woman taking a Lamaze class to prepare her for childbirth. The new part is relaxing mentally during a highly charged emotional crisis, such as the kind that visits us all in one form or another. I had this sort of experience quite unexpectedly.

During a recent health crisis I went to our local hospital for some tests. My son, Joshua, was going to be in school at the time, but my daughter, Rachel, who was 5, was home-schooled, so I made plans with my husband, Rob, to drop her off at the job where he was working so I could go to the hospital for my appointment.

Rob said he'd be praying for me during my tests; then he left for work. Later, when I arrived at his job, his truck was gone. Reg, the guy working with him, told me that my husband had gone to pick up some materials but would be back soon.

I didn't have time to wait, so I asked Reg if I could leave Rachel there with him until my husband returned. Reg agreed, but Rachel took one look at him and started crying. All the time I was getting later and later for my hospital appointment, and my frustration level was rising like the mercury in a thermometer on a hot day.

Finally I decided that the only thing I could really do was to take Rachel with me and hope for the best. I knew they wouldn't allow her to stay in the room with me because my test involved X-rays, but there was nothing I could do. At the hospital I tried several times to page Rob, but when they came to escort me into radiology he still hadn't called. The nurses kindly found a volunteer to sit with my daughter in the changing room.

For some reason Rachel accepted this, even though she didn't know the woman. So I left her there with a stranger while I submitted to painful tests to figure out what was wrong with me. While they prepped me I lay there on that cold X-ray table filled with anxiety about the tests and my health problems.

Overwhelmed with worry about having to leave Rachel with a complete stranger, I could feel the pressure inside me as I asked the "why" questions.

"Why wasn't Rob where he was supposed to be?"

"Why didn't he answer his page?"

"Why wouldn't Rachel at least stay with someone we knew?"

And I could feel anger at my husband start to crowd out everything else. But then it was as if God said, "You know what? Whatever has happened to prevent Rob from watching Rachel, it was an oversight. He didn't do it on purpose. And haven't I provided for you? I found a volunteer to watch her, and she's fine." Immediately I felt something like the release of a valve on a pressure cooker as all the anger just hissed away into nothing. *You're right, Lord,* I thought. *And I can forgive him. You've taken care of Rachel, and You'll take care of me.*

And He did. The nurse even checked on Rachel partway through my tests and informed me that my daughter was holding court in the dressing room and had all the waiting patients in stitches with stories about her brother and all his pets.

The experience illustrated to me what "being" in a trial could be like. Ultimately I would even have skipped over the frustration and anger of the beginning and gone directly to trusting God to work everything out for me in the first place. It reminds me of a story of a man who ran an orphanage. He had no food in the house, but he called all the children to the table and they said the blessing anyway. Before they had finished, someone came to the door bringing them food. God provided.

Dietrich Bonhoeffer, a young German pastor who joined the resistance in World War II and was executed by the Nazis, said, "I believe that God can and wants to create good out of everything, even evil. For that He needs people who use everything for the best. I believe that God provides us with as much strength to resist in every calamity as we need. But He does not give it in advance, so that we trust Him alone. In such a trust all anxiety about the future must be overcome."★

I agree with Bonhoeffer. Moreover, I believe this way of thinking can be perfected. First we must be "awake"—we must live in awareness. Our busyness sabotages us every day. We are too busy to be conscious of trouble before it reaches disastrous proportions. By the time we are aware that something is wrong we've crossed the line and are already at our wit's end.

Second, we must trust God to know what's best for us. "'Because the Lord disciplines those he loves, and he punishes everyone he accepts as a son.' Endure hardship as discipline; God is treating you as sons. For what son is not disciplined by his father? If you are not disciplined (and everyone undergoes discipline), then you are illegitimate children and not true sons. Moreover, we have all had human fathers who disciplined us and we respected them for it. How much more should we submit to the Father of our spirits and live! Our fathers disciplined us for a little while as they thought best; but God disciplines us for our good, that we may share in his holiness. No discipline seems pleasant at the time, but painful. Later on, however, it produces a harvest of righteousness and peace for those who have been trained by it" (Heb. 12:6-11).

Some things take time. Think what would happen if a woman who became pregnant went immediately into hard labor. Could she prepare for such a thing? Hardly. She could never relax under those circumstances. It takes nine months for a woman to get ready for labor both physically and mentally. It's a slow process because God knows that it will take her time to adjust to the changes going on in her life and that it will take time for the baby to grow and be ready to survive outside the womb.

God works long periods with us, too, preparing us for various trials, only for us to fail because we haven't been paying attention. We haven't learned the initial lessons, so when something larger comes along we fail. The bottom line is that we experience no growth. And we sit in our churches and complain about that lack of growth and ask why someone isn't doing something about it.

What we see here is the difference between armchair Christianity and practicing Christianity. I hate to say it, but it comes right back to that idea of being lukewarm. When we're lukewarm we can dress well and warm the pews and be nice when we feel like it and conform (more or less) with the two commandments: "'You shall love the Lord your God with all your heart, with all your soul, and with all your mind.' This is the first and great commandment. And the second is like it: 'You shall love your neighbor as yourself.' On these two commandments hang all the Law and the Prophets" (Matt. 22:37-40, NKJV).

We delude ourselves into a feeling of security by thinking that we can get by through keeping them nine times out of 10. We love God, after all, so that part isn't hard. We might have a tendency to skip over the whole heart, whole soul, and whole mind bit, though, because that takes some serious effort.

It's like starting an exercise program. You know it's going to be good for you, that you should be doing it. But when you actually start, it seems so hard and you get tired. It's easy to give up. That's what loving God with your whole heart, soul, and mind is like. It takes effort and commitment.

Don't get me wrong. I don't have it all down pat. But lately God has given me a glimpse of just how far I have to go to propel myself out of my armchair and into the real world of Christianity. I'm ready to try. Are you?

★ *Widerstand und ergebung, Nach Zehn Jahren: Rechenschaft an der Wende zum Jahr 1943,* pp. 20ff. As quoted at http://www.luther95.org/NELCA/inter-nos/moeller.htm.

CHAPTER 6

JOY FULL

WE NEED TO TAKE JOY SERIOUSLY, especially since we are responsible for our own. C. S. Lewis said that "joy is the serious business of heaven."[1] I think sometimes we imagine that life is the only serious business and thus we leave joy out of it completely.

If we are not full of joy, then we are missing out on the meaning of life.

But your joy can be complete. Now. Today. Not tomorrow. Not when you become the perfect Christian. Joy is not the crown of perfection or something you receive when you've got it all together as a Christian. Rather, as we have already seen, joy is the emotional fuel for the journey. If you are not filled with joy, then you are not taking advantage of all that heaven is offering you. You wouldn't take a long car trip without topping off your fuel tank. Don't live life without filling up with joy to get you to the end of the journey.

Joy begins with obedience.

Let me repeat that: Joy begins with obedience.

That's not exactly what you wanted to hear, is it? I can sympathize. Obedience is not something that comes easy to me, either. Most of my life I've been a little Goody Two-shoes with rebellious leanings. As a young Catholic I had to make up stuff to tell the priest in confession. I'm not—and I've never been—perfect by any stretch of the imagination, but for the most part I was a good kid/teen/young adult and eventually adult. I haven't knocked off any convenience stores lately. I don't kite funds. I don't even snore. Still, I have a lot of room for improvement and obedience to God's will.

It's a popular idea, embraced by Christians and non-Christians alike at times, that joy comes from "getting away with something" or doing something forbidden. But that is a lie. Going against God's will will not bring us joy. All the rewards that Satan tries to convince us will be ours by disobeying God (happiness, peace, joy, satisfaction, contentment, and even pleasure) are the same ones he tempted Adam and Eve with in the garden. Nothing has changed.

God created everything in an orderly fashion. There are reasons for the ways things work, and most of them are logical to our minds. The parts that don't immediately make sense to us just demonstrate our limitations when it comes to trying to understand the divine mind. But divine order exists in everything from heaven to space to the biology of all living things to the sanctuary setup. God has a plan for everything. Not leaving us to the mercy of chance, He has provided essential guidelines for every important area of life. The product of our obedience to that order (and not following our own selfish desires) is joy.

What are we to be obedient to? God's precepts. David tells us in Psalm 119:111: "Your statutes are my heritage forever; they are the joy of my heart." God's commandments are our joy. When we keep them, we follow Him and receive His best for our lives. Not second best, or third best, or the leftovers, or the stuff we scrape off the bottom of the barrel after we've gone our own way and messed things up.

Ellen White observed that "we are to have Christ's joy, and His greatest joy was to see men obeying the truth. Can we desire more than this? 'Greater works than these shall ye do,' the Savior said, 'because I go unto my Father.' He who truly believes this promise can never be halfhearted in the service of Christ. May the God of heaven tear away the veil that dims our perception and hinders us from discerning His requirements and from following Christ. O that by living faith we would grasp the hand of infinite Power, receiving strength to work His works. This it is our privilege to do. If we will take Christ at His word, He will be honored and glorified, and we shall be partakers of His joy."[2]

Not long ago my husband was reading from the *Bible Story* books to our children, and I listened while I sketched Angus, our Cairn terrier, who had stretched out by the fire. The story concerned Saul's attempts on David's life. Here's the part I thought was interesting: "He wanted to see the man of God who had anointed him. Life had become such a muddle. He had tried so hard to do right, and now all this trouble had come to him. He wondered why, and what he should do next. . . . Just what Samuel said to David we do not know, but we can be sure he told him to be patient and to trust God to work everything out right in the end."[3]

David was following God's commands—doing what was right. Still he was in a terrible pickle. We can look at him and wonder, *Where was his joy?* Surely he did not have joy when Saul hurled a javelin at him. Or did he? David was not suffering from a guilty conscience—not at this point in his life, anyway. He was not looking for what he could get *now,* but was counting on what God promised him in the *future.*

We have to remember that when things are not going right

down here, despite our best efforts, relying on God for the future and continuing in obedience to Him will give us joy in the here and now. And that joy will sustain us.

If joy begins with obedience, it continues when we realize that God is always working out His purposes through all our circumstances, even the difficult ones. The Lord did not abandon David, and He will not desert us. We are to "count it all joy when [we] fall into various trials" (James 1:2, NKJV). Why? Because "we know that all things work together for good to those who love God, to those who are the called according to His purpose" (Rom. 8:28, NKJV). Even when you miss your flight.

Having finished speaking at my first women's retreat, I was happy but tired and missed my family. My ride was late getting to the airport, but my flight wasn't scheduled to depart for another 10 minutes. Although I knew it was close, I wasn't really worried—until the woman at the United Airlines counter told me I couldn't get on the plane.

"I'm sorry," she said, not sounding the least bit apologetic. "There's a 15-minute cutoff for that flight."

Secretly I didn't want to get on that plane in the first place. I had seen robins larger than the two aircraft I had flown over on. But while I wasn't exactly looking forward to making the same nauseating flights in reverse, it was my only way home.

"All our flights are booked until Tuesday," she added helpfully.

Somehow I couldn't absorb the fact that I wouldn't get home for at least two days. I had used up all my energy at the women's retreat and had nothing left to cope with this disaster. In my mind I was standing before God, my mouth hanging open, saying, "How could this possibly happen?"

Printing out my ticket, she suggested that I try other airlines to see if they would accept it, let me pay the difference, and give me a seat on one of their planes. I tried US Airways. The woman there couldn't find any seats unless I wanted to pay an additional $1,000 to exchange my ticket. I would have, but I didn't have the money. But she did tell me that she saw a United Airlines flight the next morning out of Dulles going to my destination that was only half full. I could book a United flight to Dulles that night, stay over, and try to board that half-full plane in the morning.

When I returned to the United counter I saw that a line had suddenly formed in front of it. "Let's try another airline," urged the woman who had driven me to the airport.

It was that or stand in line. We approached the Delta counter. "I'm sure this is a futile question, but would you take my ticket and give me a ride home?" I told the attendant where I wanted to go and then heard the sweetest words on earth.

"I can get you home today."

"How much will it cost me?"

"Nothing," she replied. "I'll just take your United ticket."

Incredible! That alone would have been an enormous blessing, but God wasn't finished with me yet. Not only did He get me home that night; He got me on *bigger planes* so that I didn't get sick. Once aboard the Delta flight, I felt gratitude overwhelming me. Again I realized how much energy we waste being upset about things that are really going to end up blessing us in the end. While we won't see every blessing that comes disguised as a disaster, I thank God for letting me recognize this one. It gave me a new perspective on the relativity of our circumstances.

We may not have happiness during a trial, but we can have joy by reminding ourselves that the experience is temporary and that God has a purpose for whatever we are going through or He would not allow it to happen to us. "No temptation has overtaken you except such as is common to man; but God is faithful, who will not allow you to be tempted beyond what you are able, but with the temptation will also make the way of escape, that you may be able to bear it" (1 Cor. 10:13, NKJV).

God realizes that we will become discouraged in the midst of a trial. But He also knows, better than we ever can, that anything we go through is fleeting! Paul tells us: "Therefore we do not lose heart. Even though our outward man is perishing, yet the inward man is being renewed day by day. For our light affliction, which is but for a moment, is working for us a far more exceeding and eternal weight of glory, while we do not look at the things which are seen, but at the things which are not seen. For the things which are seen are temporary, but the things which are not seen are eternal" (2 Cor. 4:16-18, NKJV).

The renewal Paul is talking about is joy. As we overcome in each trial, it strengthens our joy, leading us to respond in obedience and trust God with every detail of our life. He is in control, and we follow Him. Following Him results in joy, because we are filled with the Spirit. And when we are filled with the Spirit, it will be obvious to everyone. We will be "speaking to one another in psalms and hymns and spiritual songs, singing and making melody in [our] heart to the Lord, giving thanks always for all things to God the Father in the name of our Lord Jesus Christ, submitting to one another in the fear of God" (Eph. 5:19-21, NKJV).

A direct connection exists between being filled with the Holy Spirit and joy. Scripture lists joy as the second fruit of the Spirit. "But the fruit of the Spirit is love, *joy* . . ." (Gal. 5:22, NKJV). Joy results from being filled with the Spirit. And the Spirit will touch and influence everything around us.

I was inspired recently by a Marianne Williamson quote. "Our deepest fear is not that we are inadequate. Our deepest fear is that we are powerful beyond measure. It is our light, not our darkness, that most frightens us. We ask ourselves, Who am

I to be brilliant, gorgeous, talented, fabulous? Actually, who are you *not* to be? You are a child of God. Your playing small does not serve the world. There is nothing enlightened about shrinking so that other people won't feel insecure around you. . . . We were born to make manifest the glory of God that is within us. It is not just in some of us; it is in everyone. And as we let our own light shine, we unconsciously give others permission to do the same. We are liberated from our own fear, our presence automatically liberates others."[4]

It's so easy to be falsely modest. We don't want to call attention to ourselves or our accomplishments. Instead, we're supposed to wait for someone else to do that, right? There's a fine line between tooting your own horn and being up-front about your commendable actions. No need to break your arm patting yourself on the back, but on the other hand, if no one knows what you are doing, whom are you really glorifying?

I used to feel that way about donating blood. Giving your own blood to save the life of someone else has always seemed such a noble gesture to me. As soon as I was old enough I signed up to donate at my school. I was so determined to give blood that I wore my dad's old Army jacket and hid rocks and stuff in the pockets because I knew I didn't meet the weight requirement. From then on I gave blood regularly until my first pregnancy. But I rarely talked about it. It seemed like bragging somehow.

Then, years later, when I hadn't donated blood in years, someone mentioned to me that they had given blood on their lunch break. My first thought was not *Oh, don't you think you're special* but *What a wonderful thing!* Then I immediately thought, *I should see when the next blood drive is in my area.* If the person who had donated blood had not mentioned it to me I would not have looked into giving it myself. Not only were they not seeking glory; they in fact inspired me to donate as well.

I've had this same experience with other charitable efforts. Through the years I've contributed to dinners for the homeless, done pet therapy for the aged, cooked for and socialized with prisoners returning to society, made teddy bears for disadvantaged children, donated food to food shelves, and other things. Whenever I mention my activities to people the result is often "That's a great idea! How can I get involved?"

After giving the matter some consideration, I've come to the conclusion that it's the spirit with which you offer the information that makes the difference. For example, early in my career whenever I met people I used to look for opportunities to mention that I wrote for a living. After all, I enjoyed getting a pat on the back. Writing is an interesting career, and most of the time people peppered me with questions about it. It made me feel important.

Then God brought it to my attention that the motives behind bringing up what I did were misguided. I didn't need people to tell me that my career was valuable and that I was doing a great work. God would give me all the reassurance I needed on that score. And He found creative ways to do it, too. One unique way He does this is that whenever I become discouraged about writing, people I don't know start e-mailing me and telling me how something I've written has changed their life. They ask me to please not stop writing, which is usually exactly what I have been thinking about doing in my discouragement, which has led me to feel that the sacrifices of my career outweigh any benefits. Such e-mail encouragement has happened so many times now that when an e-mail comes my husband immediately asks me if I'm discouraged!

One of the embarrassing things I realized was that I was so busy formulating answers to the questions I was sure people would ask me when they found out about my writing that I rarely posed any questions about them. If they did offer any information about themselves, I didn't retain it, because I wasn't paying attention to what they were saying; I was focused on what I was going to say.

Once I realized what I was doing, I made a conscious effort not to mention what I did. If someone asked me, I'd answer, but I rarely volunteered the information. I'm pretty good at it now. And people find out anyway. Not long ago I turned up at a non-denominational women's Bible study, and the leader exclaimed, "Hey, you're famous!"

"I am?" I said.

"Yes," she explained, "you write books, and someone I know who isn't even a Christian read one of them!" God has a way of leading people to that knowledge if it will benefit them.

The spirit in which we offer the information is more important than the content itself—at least insofar as we are concerned.

It's important for us to share the joy we have. The lack of joy in people's hearts today is why you see Columbine and Oklahoma City and the Trade Center attack and the Washington, D.C., area snipers. When you don't have joy, you feel that nothing better will come in the end. When you do have it, it makes all the difference.

I don't need to tell you what a life of hopelessness looks like. You can turn on CNN, listen to NPR, or read a newspaper and observe what happens. Some Christians debate about how bad it's got to get before Jesus comes back. Will it be as bad as Noah's day? as bad as Sodom and Gomorrah? When is "bad" bad enough? If you ask the parents of any abducted and murdered child, or the friends of sniper victims, or soldiers fighting in Afghanistan, or neighbors in a gang-run neighborhood, or a cancer patient, they'll all tell you that it's plenty bad enough. God's not waiting for it to get worse. Any atrocity is "bad enough."

Rather, I believe, God is waiting for us—waiting for His people to live out the joy He's placed in their lives and share that joy with others. He doesn't want to lose anyone. When the *Titanic* went down, hundreds of people perished. It's a well-known fact that the ship did not have enough lifeboats to save everyone, but many of those people didn't perish for lack of lifeboats. The lifeboats were not completely filled. Passengers drowned for lack of *getting into* the lifeboats.

Jesus gave us the commission: "Go into all the world and preach the good news to all creation" (Mark 16:15). He gave us the joy—the fuel—to accomplish His mission. It's your responsibility and mine to go into our world and tell the good news of the gospel of Christ. Many assume that it is the pastor's job. But pastors can only do so much. If it were only the clergy's job, Jesus would have said, "Support your pastors as they go into all the world." But He didn't. He simply declared "Go."

Also, it's interesting that He didn't say, "If you feel like it, you could go into all the world" or "You can send satellites into all the world" or even "If you feel called to be a missionary, you can go into all the world." The command was just "Go."

We don't even have to travel far. The world is all around us. Very few of us live in remote areas where the nearest neighbor is 50 miles away. Some of us might have 50 neighbors in the very building we live in. Even if you somehow don't have neighbors, you work with people, you see people at the grocery store, you have family. Should you by the wildest stretch of the imagination live in a single room and never come out, you probably have a telephone. We're all connected to other people in some way. That's the part of the "world" we're responsible for.

And we've got time. Let's think about this for a minute. What's going on in your world? Can you think of anyone you see on a regular basis who does not know Jesus? Write down anyone who comes to mind:

_____   _____

_____   _____

_____   _____

_____   _____

_____   _____

These people are your commission. Jesus said "Go!" The *Titanic* is sinking. Each of them needs to get into a lifeboat, or they will perish. You know where the lifeboats are! You can help them find the Lifeboat! But each case will be different. What works for one person will not persuade another. If you can't think of a way to reach the people on your list, pray about it, because God knows how to help those people. He knows how to enable you to fulfill the commission He gave you. Not only that, but He desires to take us home to heaven with Him more than we want Him to come. But He longs to have those individuals you listed above waiting with you when He gets here.

So what are you waiting for? "Go into all the world and preach the good news to all creation."

[1] Quoted in John Ortberg, *The Life You've Always Wanted*.

[2] Ellen G. White, "That Your Joy Might Be Full," *Signs of the Times,* Aug. 11, 1909.

[3] Arthur S. Maxwell, *The Bible Story* (Washington, D.C.: Review and Herald Pub. Assn., 1975), vol. 4, p. 20.

[4] Marianne Williamson, *A Return to Love* (New York: HarperCollins, 1992), pp. 190, 1901.

CHAPTER 7

CREATING A JOY-FILLED LIFE

A **JOY-FILLED LIFE DOESN'T JUST HAPPEN.** It would be nice if it did. Jesus gave us His joy, so unless He tells us otherwise, I think we can safely assume that we're all filled with that joy. I have it as I type these words, and you have it as you read them. It was a free gift to us from God. But in the same way we tend a garden to prevent weeds from taking over, our joy is something that we must carefully guard and cultivate.

Simply defined, joy is God's presence in our lives, which implants in us a living hope for the future. It allows us to live each moment, no matter what it brings, in a godly way, because we know that whatever circumstance befalls us is only temporary and that a much greater life awaits us. OK, maybe that wasn't such a simple definition, but I think that crystallizes the essence of this book. If you take nothing away but that definition and the rest of this chapter, I believe you'll find your life greatly enriched.

So we need to guard and cultivate joy. How do we go about doing that? Joy gets compromised and even destroyed in the various ways we listed earlier (see chapter 4). We need to protect ourselves against such situations. Now, before you throw up your hands and sputter, "Yeah, but you don't understand what I'm dealing with," let me hasten to add that no matter how hard we try, we'll still find ourselves in the kinds of situations we have previously discussed. Just because we are aware of the pitfalls doesn't mean we won't occasionally land in one.

Look at David. I hardly think he was looking for persecution from Saul, but there wasn't a whole lot he could do about it, either. *Just because we find ourselves in a situation that compromises our joy does not mean we will lose it.* In fact, the opposite is often the case—our joy sustains us in our difficult times. Which is as it should be.

But guarding our joy during times that we find ourselves overwhelmed with life's situations becomes proactive, which means that we must actively cultivate joy. By doing so, we will refresh the means that God has for sustaining us during hard times.

Try explaining to a child sometime how it is that God comforts us during sad times. Children can see how He protects us as, for example, we go through a dangerous situation and emerge unharmed or pray for protection during a trip and reach our destination without incident. God protects us so that we remain unhurt. He leads us when He shows us through His written word what to do. These are things a child, or anybody else, can see. They are tangible. But comfort is intangible.

Many times I have wondered how God comforts us. I find that reading His words is reassuring, but then I am language-oriented. Words mean a lot to me. I find the poetry of the Bible very consoling, which perhaps explains why I like the book of Psalms best. Still, God is not a physical presence. He cannot wrap His arms around us literally. But when our joy is strong it is like an internal hug from God and has the same effect. It points us toward better times ahead. Isn't that what comfort is all about?

JOY

There are many ways to cultivate joy. I'll go through the ones that occur to me, but I encourage you to take a few moments at the end of this chapter to come up with some others and to think of some examples of how God has refreshed your joy lately in ways that maybe you hadn't realized until you read this.

Pray

I suppose this one is obvious to you, but I will admit that it's often the last one I think of. I get so wrapped up in a solution that I fixate on what needs to be done to reach it. It's almost as if I have blinders on. Fortunately, my children, especially Joshua, have given me a wake-up call in this area many times. For Josh, the *first* thing you should do in any situation is pray. He is a wonderful example to me.

God wants us to pray for joy. He knows where we should go and how we should get there, and He knows how to preserve our joy on the journey. "You will show me the path of life; in Your presence is fullness of joy; at Your right hand are pleasures forevermore" (Ps. 16:11, NKJV).

Jesus prayed for joy, believe it or not, in Gethsemane. "No," you may say, "I don't think so. How could He even have expected joy?" But remember that Jesus endured the cross "for the joy set before him" (Heb. 12:2). What did Jesus pray for when He was in Gethsemane preparing to face the cross? "O My Father, if it is possible, let this cup pass from Me; nevertheless, *not as I will, but as You will*" (Matt. 26:39, NKJV). Jesus prayed to know His Father's will for His situation. Doing His Father's will, then, was the means by which He acquired His joy.

We can apply this today by actively seeking to know God's will for our lives and then doing it. One of the ways we can accomplish this is through prayer. We pray for all kinds of things, but let's especially pray to know God's heart. We can put the grocery list of requests to one side for now and concentrate on getting intimate with God. The result of following God's will is joy.

About a year ago some friends of mine were struggling without water when their well went dry during a drought. Month after month they made do with no running water. The family included six people at the time, and their predicament quickly got old. My friend e-mailed me and said, "I've been praying about it, but I must be asking for the wrong thing, because I'm not getting a yes."

It's easy to assume that if we don't receive an obvious positive response to our prayers, then something is wrong. That's not necessarily the case. We may just be looking in the wrong place for an answer. "You might be getting a yes to the prayer you're not asking," I e-mailed back. "Perhaps it's 'Give me faith that You'll take care of the water' and you're getting a yes to that. It's maybe a little scary how we don't get the answers we're looking for sometimes.

"We started a prayer notebook in school to keep track of our prayer requests. The first on the list was for Squeak's leg (Josh's mouse had some paralysis in her leg last week, and we didn't know why; we brought her to the vet, who said she'd probably have to live with it). Now she's using it again, and all is well—prayer answered with a big YES. The next was for a young girl fighting for her life, the friend of a friend. She died on Thursday. Prayer answered with a big NO.

"Your well is the next thing written on the list. To the right are spaces to record answers. I had to write 'Yes' to Squeak's leg and 'Passed away' near the young girl's name. God heals a mouse and takes a young girl with her whole life ahead of her.

"What kind of sense can we make of that? None. Except that while we need to ask for what we want, at the same time we need to prepare for what God gives. And it's not always what we want. Maybe the best prayer is 'Help me to accept what You want for my life and help me to want it too.'"

Job, who knew a thing or two about disappointment and pain, nevertheless believed that God would fill us with joy if we prayed. "He shall pray to God, and He will delight in him, he shall see His face with joy, for He restores to man His righteousness. Then he looks at men and says, 'I have sinned, and perverted what was right, and it did not profit me.' He will redeem his soul from going down to the Pit, and his life shall see the light" (Job 33:26-28, NKJV). In the end our life will see the light.

A pastor once said to me, "Open up to the possibilities. God wants to love you extravagantly. Don't limit Him with what you think you need—let Him show you how much He can give you."

I think we can apply this to every situation, every prayer. Open yourself up to the possibilities. "Now to Him who is able to do exceedingly abundantly above all that we ask or think, according to the power that works in us, to Him be glory in the church by Christ Jesus to all generations, forever and ever. Amen" (Eph. 3:20, 21, NKJV).

Practice awareness of God

It's been said that nature is God's second book. If His first book, the Bible, is a revelation of His great love for us, what does His second book say? I think it does what any good sequel should do—it continues the theme of the first book. When you observe a magnificent sunset or a canopy of stars on a dark night or a newly hatched chick or a soaring eagle, what are you really seeing? All of nature has God's fingerprint on it. He created all of it for us to enjoy. It all says, "I love you."

I like the "God Speaks" billboards springing up all over the country. The campaign originated at the Smith Agency, and reportedly an anonymous individual is paying for them. We don't have any billboards yet in Vermont, but I have seen a few while traveling. Here are some of my favorites:

"'What part of "Thou shalt not . . ." didn't you understand?'—God."

"'We need to talk.'—God."

"'That "Love Thy Neighbor" thing . . . I meant it.'—God."

"'My way is the highway.'—God."

"'Don't make Me come down there.'—God."

While they may give us a chuckle (and occasionally hit home), what they do better is to remind us that messages from God exist all around us, but they aren't plastered on a billboard—and we miss many of them. A billboard is a pretty obvious way to get a message across, but God doesn't often use them to communicate with us. His messages are more subtle. Because of earth's fallen nature we may have trouble recognizing them. "Now we see but a poor reflection as in a mirror; then we shall see face to face. Now I know in part; then I shall know fully, even as I am fully known" (1 Cor. 13:12).

I've had many practical—even some extraordinary—experiences with this. One such time I was out walking. It was early enough that I passed several groups of children waiting for their buses. It was fall, and I was struggling with depression and fatigue. Because exercise is beneficial for depression, I try to go out every day. Normally I thrive on exercise, but at this time I was still recovering from knee surgery, and walking was painful as well as inconvenient.

The route I follow includes a desolate stretch with no houses in sight, but lots of trees. I always bring my black Lab with me, but he isn't much protection, being a pushover when it comes to aggression of any kind. So I usually tense up and walk faster through that stretch.

One morning as we approached the far end of this segment I saw something colorful on the road. My first thought was that someone had dropped some garbage out of a car. As I drew closer I started to make out what seemed to be a flower. Sure enough, it was a silk rose, placed right there on the road where I couldn't possibly miss it. I still have no idea how it got there at that exact spot to brighten my day unless God reached down and placed it there. I still have it to remind me that God cares about us at all times and that He has amazing ways to reassure us of that fact, but someday I'm going to liberate it to enrich someone else's life.

When you start to look for such "love notes" from God, you'll be amazed at how many you will find. It can be something as simple as finding a parking spot when you're in a rush to something as elaborate as a long-lost friend showing up to renew an acquaintance you've sorely missed. The secular world would regard them as coincidences, but because we know God we can recognize them for what they really are: God's reminders that He loves us and cares deeply for every tiny aspect of our lives. Such things show us that nothing is beneath His notice, and therefore nothing we are concerned about is beyond His attention either. We can and should take all of our concerns to Him, big or small, because He cares for us and wants to help us.

Praise

At heart I suppose we're all either pessimists or optimists. I don't think there's any middle ground on this issue. I've yet to meet anyone who was half-and-half (but then, I'm young and there's still time). To illustrate my theory, let's use my husband and me as examples. I would be the optimist in this case, and he would be the pessimist (though I think he'd probably prefer the term *realist*).

Let's say we decide to go on a canoe trip in a month. I immediately start to visualize all the fun we're going to have. In my picture the sun is shining, the temperature is perfect, and there are no bugs. My husband, on the other hand, begins to dish up pessimism. There will be bugs, it might rain, and it will probably be cold at least at night, so we'd better pack warm.

Chances are decent that the actual trip will be better than my husband expects, and because his expectations are low, he will have a more enjoyable time than he anticipates. However, the possibility also exists that it will be worse than I anticipate, which means I will have a worse time than I imagine I will. Because my expectations are high, I will probably be disappointed.

I've heard people argue in favor of keeping your expectations low just so you won't be disappointed, but I don't like that idea. Yes, it's true that the less you expect, the less you will experience disappointment, but consider the alternative. The more you expect, the more you will achieve. In short, if you keep your expectations up, you might be disappointed more often, but you will go further than if you keep them low.

The same holds true with joy. Sure, we can approach every situation expecting a negative outcome, but where is our God in that situation? Is He that small? A friend of mine once said that if we start out looking at the problem and then praise God, we'll see the problem as large and God as small. But if we start out praising the Lord, the problem will appear small next to our awesome God. We've got to come at things from the right perspective. Thus we must praise God first and trust that He is in control and that He'll work everything out in His own time, in His own way. All we've got to do is to follow Him.

This is particularly true during hard times. One of the many paradoxes of the Christian life is that the harder the going gets, the more joyful we can become by praising God and trusting that He will deliver us. The Bible declares that "the joy of the

Lord is your strength" (Neh. 8:10, NKJV). And David, who knew a lot about persecution, said: "And now my head shall be lifted up above my enemies all around me; therefore I will offer sacrifices of joy in His tabernacle; I will sing, yes, I will sing praises to the Lord" (Ps. 27:6, NKJV).

Does this mean we'll *feel* like praising God? Not necessarily. But it is a well-known fact that feelings follow actions, so we might actually end up feeling like it. However, we can't rely on our emotions to prompt us to praise God during tough times. We should remember that "weeping may endure for a night, but joy comes in the morning" (Ps. 30:5, NKJV). I'm by no means a Bible scholar, but the Hebrew for "joy comes" in this passage is number 7440 in *Strong's Concordance,* and its translation is: *"rinnâh* . . . i.e., shout of joy or grief—cry, gladness, joy, proclamation, rejoicing, shouting, sing (-ing), triumph." [1] One could translate the passage this way: "Weeping may *endure* **stay** for *a night* **an evening,** but *joy cometh* **shouting** in the morning." [2] I like that. Joy comes shouting in the morning! What a glorious word picture.

Not many people feel happy when they are weeping, unless they are crying *because* they are happy. But no matter their feelings at the time, joy will follow their sorrow, gladness their sadness. Each and every trial or circumstance with its pain and suffering then becomes an object lesson. More than anything, such times should remind us that life won't always be like this. Our lasting hope comes in the morning. "Those who sow in tears shall reap in joy" (Ps. 126:5, NKJV).

Celebrate

Israel threw a lot of parties in its day, and do you know what most of them were about? They were celebrations of remembrance. Consider Purim. After the Jews received the decree proclaiming that they could defend themselves against their enemies, "Mordecai recorded these events, and he sent letters to all the Jews throughout the provinces of King Xerxes, near and far, to have them celebrate annually the fourteenth and fifteenth days of the month of Adar as the time when the Jews got relief from their enemies, and as the month when their sorrow was turned into joy and their mourning into a day of celebration.

"He wrote them to observe the days as days of feasting and joy and giving presents of food to one another and gifts to the poor. So the Jews agreed to continue the celebration they had begun, doing what Mordecai had written to them. For Haman son of Hammedatha, the Agagite, the enemy of all the Jews, had plotted against the Jews to destroy them and had cast the *pur* (that is, the lot) for their ruin and destruction. But when the plot came to the king's attention, he issued written orders that the evil scheme Haman had devised against the Jews should come back onto his own head, and that he and his sons should be hanged on the gallows. (Therefore these days were called Purim, from the word *pur*.)

"Because of everything written in this letter and because of what they had seen and what had happened to them, the Jews took it upon themselves to establish the custom that they and their descendants and all who join them should without fail observe these two days every year, in the way prescribed and at the time appointed. These days should be remembered and observed in every generation by every family, and in every province and in every city. And these days of Purim should never cease to be celebrated by the Jews, nor should the memory of them die out among their descendants" (Esther 9:20-28).

Other celebrations include Sukkoth, which commemorates the 40 years when the children of Israel wandered in the wilderness and lived in temporary shelters. Shavuot, or Pentecost, memorializes the giving of the Torah. Passover freed the Jews from physical bondage. Rosh Hodesh began the new month. The day after the sighting of a new moon the people had a festival. Hanukkah celebrates the miracle of the oil at the rededication of the Temple. The oil was supposed to burn throughout the night every night, but not much remained that hadn't been defiled by the Greeks. Miraculously, the available oil burned for eight days, the length of time needed to make a fresh supply.

In our own life we have many reasons to celebrate. I recently wrote two books on the celebrations of Adventists: *Adventist Family Traditions* and *Making Holidays Special*. Both books talk about the need for celebration in our lives. "Adventist family traditions are relatively new as traditions go, since Adventism as a religion has existed for only a century and a half. Nonetheless, some of our traditions are distinct and unique. They set us apart and mark us as a group of like believers. Some of these traditions are passed on from one generation to the next. Some of them are particular to an ethnic group, a region, or even a church body, but many of them are recognizable to anyone in the church, regardless of origin.

"Are these traditions important? I believe so. They accomplish two very special tasks. First, they bind us to God by reinforcing our relationship to Him in a pattern of continuity. Second, they bind us to each other in solidarity, giving us the shared experiences of a group having common goals, beliefs and practices. Our traditions are important because they anchor us to the past and keep us secure against an unknown future. They provide stability in times of change and uncertainty."[3]

Celebration refreshes joy by giving us the opportunity to express our gratitude for all the wonderful things that God has done and continues to do in our lives. Sabbath is a mini weekly celebration of this fact. "Through the chaos of everyday life the

Sabbath shines like a beacon, pointing straight to God, reminding us that He is in control. He was in control at Creation, He was in control at the cross, and our future is in His hands. We have nothing to fear. No matter what happens here on earth, God is in control of this world, working out His plan and purpose."[4]

We wouldn't dream of going a year, a month, a week, or even a day without telling the people closest to us how much we love them. When they have a birthday, anniversary, or other special occasion we plan a big party and do all manner of things to show them how much we love and appreciate them. Don't we have even more reason to celebrate God and what He's doing in our lives?

All of us have plenty of opportunities during the year to celebrate life. Think of all the holidays we observe as a matter of course. In the United States we honor July 4 as the day we won our independence. In France they celebrate the same thing on July 14. Much of the world treats January 1 as the beginning of the new year. Some countries have a thanksgiving day. It's not hard to find a commemoration in every month of the year.

So why can't we apply that same principle to spiritual things? Let's not only find the time to celebrate all that God is doing for us, but do it with joy. Turn a blind eye to marketing hype and don't buy into the secular spin on established holidays. Take the time to remember and talk about the real reason behind them. And when there is no holiday, celebrate anyway. It strengthens joy.

Cultivate gratitude

We've already discussed some ways to cultivate gratitude, but there are many more. One way involves sharing with others. The very act of sharing is an acknowledgment that we have been blessed abundantly and that we should bestow blessings on others in the same manner. "Give, and it will be given to you: good measure, pressed down, shaken together, and running over will be put into your bosom. For with the same measure that you use, it will be measured back to you" (Luke 6:38, NKJV). It is our responsibility to pass our blessings on.

There are endless ways to share. I don't have in mind simply "he who has two tunics, let him give to him who has none; and he who has food, let him do likewise" (Luke 3:11, NKJV).

That is certainly one way to go about it. But what I'm talking about is more of an ongoing, daily kind that requires keeping your eyes and ears open to what's happening around you and considering how it could benefit someone else. Perhaps you are at a library book sale and while browsing you find a book that is just the kind of thing a friend would love to own. So you spend the 50 cents, buy the book, and mail it with a short note or drop it by the person's house later. You have shared your joy, acknowledging that God has blessed you exceedingly. And monetarily it cost you only 50 cents! That's the great thing about sharing God's blessings. They don't have to cost much. It's truly the thought that counts.

Countless ways exist for you to share your joy. One is simply to write a short note to a person you love. Alexandra Stoddard, a well-known interior designer, says we should hand-write a note to someone every day. "A variety of notepapers and cards can make letter writing more efficient and fun. If you are thanking someone for dinner you might select a museum post-card of a feast. If you send one note a day you'll need 365 a year, so you should collect stationery and postcards as you go along. Have a pretty cup to hold some colored pens so you can have plenty of variety when you sit down to write. The letter-writing ritual should be generously provided for. Sending a surprise letter to a friend is like sending your ship out to sail."[5] Not only will the person who receives the note be blessed, but so will you for sharing.

If you are a tactile person, as I am, you'll receive joy simply from handling the paper and writing your words with a fountain pen. Pausing for this small ritual, you'll be, almost unconsciously, counting your blessings. To deepen the experience, you can say a short prayer for whomever you are writing to each day. Think of all the prayers you'll have prayed at the end of a year and practically without giving it a thought. We often put off prayers because we're too busy to pray, but saying a prayer while you address an envelope takes no extra time at all.

Another way you can bless others and pass along your joy is to think of them as you go through your day. We often see things that others would benefit from: a magazine or newspaper article, a bar of soap or a package of note cards when we are shopping—even the samples that come in junk mail or magazines could be useful or enjoyable to someone we know. Rather than waiting for a birthday or special occasion, pop such things into the mail or hand-deliver them to brighten someone's day. You never know the kind of impact it will have. When the Holy Spirit prompts you to bless someone in this way, follow the Nike ad's advice and "just do it."

Look at the big picture

One of the most basic things that joy requires is that we view the big picture. It's not enough to look at the present and base our actions on that. We must glance ahead, toward the goal, and base our actions on the potential reward. "Do you not know that those who run in a race all run, but one receives the prize? Run in such a way that you may obtain it. And everyone who competes for the prize is temperate in all things. Now they do it to obtain a perishable crown, but we for an imperishable crown" (1 Cor. 9:24, 25, NKJV).

JOY

At a recent women's Bible study we were discussing the concept of finding joy in trials. I asked if anyone had actually managed to do that while still in the situation rather than afterward. Kay reported that she'd had some success if she had immediately stopped her automatic thought responses and purposefully changed them to godly thought responses. For example, if her husband did something that upset her that in turn made her start to catalog mentally all the reasons he was a "miserable so-and-so," she forced herself to stop and say, "I am upset right now, but that doesn't mean that I don't love my husband or that he's not a good man. I am responsible for my own attitudes. God, help me to react in a loving way to my husband and enable me to work this situation out."

After that, Kay explained, she was able to apologize to her husband if she had said anything in anger. She also reported that her attitude influenced how her husband responded to the situation as well. What we don't often consider is that we're all interconnected, bouncing around and against each other like so many billiard balls. We can't "run into" anyone without producing an effect. Imagine what it would be like if, rather than crashing into each other helter-skelter all the time, more or less out of control, we could gently "bump" into each other in a way that would actually help the other person come closer to reaching their goal. But, of course, we can imagine what that would be like. And when we do that, we are "loving one another," as Jesus said. "This is My commandment, that you love one another as I have loved you" (John 15:12, NKJV).

If we intend to overcome our tendency to be shortsighted and instead focus on the long-term goal that awaits us, we need to be *constantly* in contact with God through the Holy Spirit. Without that continual empowering we wouldn't be able to look ahead—we'd be mired right where we stood.

CREATING A JOY-FILLED LIFE

As you can see, there are many ways to cultivate joy. I hope that my experience has shown you some ways that hadn't occurred to you. I encourage you to take a few minutes and write down others that you might think of and then to make them a part of your daily life.

Other ways to cultivate joy:

_____

_____

_____

_____

_____

How God has refreshed my joy in the past:

_____

_____

_____

[1] James Strong, *Strong's Exhaustive Concordance of the Bible* (Grandville, Mich.: World Bible Publishers, 1986).

[2] Herb Jahn, *Exegeses Ready Research Bible* (Grandville, Mich.: World Bible Publishers, 1993).

[3] Celeste perrino Walker, *Adventist Family Traditions* (Nampa, Idaho: Pacific Press Pub. Assn., 2002), p. 5.

[4] Walker, *Making Sabbath Special* (Nampa, Idaho: Pacific Press Pub. Assn., 1999), p. 29.

[5] Alexandra Stoddard, *Living a Beautiful Life* (New York: Avon Books, 1986), pp. 32, 33.

CHAPTER 8

SHARING JOY

SHARING RELIGION AND SHARING JOY are not the same. While there is nothing wrong with offering our beliefs to others, if we do it at the expense of sharing Christ we commit a grave error. Our job isn't to go out into the world and convert people to Adventism. Rather, our responsibility is to lead them to the Savior. He'll take care of their denomination.

Our joy, our hope, our Savior, is what people should notice in us. It will be what draws them to us. If we short-circuit their interest by homing in on a recital of our beliefs, we will lose them. They don't care if we can accurately interpret prophecy, don't wear jewelry, or are strict vegetarians. What they do want to know is why we have joy. It's our job to tell them. But we have to have something to offer them in the first place.

Back when I was a newer Adventist than I am now, I had trouble with this concept. I just couldn't understand how I could be friends with someone who didn't also have my beliefs. Partly I was afraid that since I hadn't had my beliefs all that long I'd somehow absorb those of the other person. It was a real problem because there weren't a lot of individuals my age in my local congregation.

SHARING JOY

Although I got along fine with the people I met at my job at a bank, my religion always made me "privileged" because I got to leave work early on Fridays and if any emergency calls came in on Saturday I was not on the list to head up the mountain and unjam the ATM machine or fill it if it ran out of bills during a busy weekend. People at work were nice to me, but I was strange to them. I wouldn't go out with them to the bars. I wouldn't swear. I ate funny stuff at lunch. They couldn't understand me, because I didn't fit into their world.

When I finally did find some Christian friends, they didn't share my religion, and I immediately went into the "seek and convert" mode. To me, my response was obvious. After all, they weren't Adventists, so therefore their theology was wrong and it was my obligation as a member in good standing of the Adventist Church to correct the error of their beliefs. Wasn't it? Well, wasn't it? I started by opening up discussions of theology that led to "What do you believe about . . . ?" (most of which I already knew because of my association with a number of religions before becoming an Adventist in the first place).

My question would quickly be followed (most times before the air even fully left their lungs at the end of their answer) with "Well, we believe . . . because the Bible says . . ." Would you believe that not once, to my knowledge, did I ever change someone's mind about their theology in this manner? I couldn't believe it either. I thought that perhaps my approach needed work, so I practiced more often. Somehow I hope that the Holy Spirit was able to use my testimony despite myself, but I imagine I probably did more harm than good. I should have followed Paul's advice to Timothy: "And the servant of the Lord must not strive; but be gentle unto all men, apt to teach, patient, in meekness instructing those that oppose themselves; if God peradventure will give them repentance to the acknowledging of the truth; and that they may recover themselves out of the snare of the devil, who are taken captive by him at his will" (2 Tim. 2:24-26, KJV).

These days I have lots of non-Adventist friends, and while I haven't yet converted any of them, I have discovered how to appreciate their Christianity and their relationship with Christ and how it works. As far as I know, their theology hasn't warped me yet, but in many cases their sincere relationship with Christ has strengthened my own. Through the years I have answered a lot of questions about Adventism, and I try to do it without bringing up all the lifestyle issues first, though they are the most obvious to an outsider. Lifestyle isn't what's going to save us. Christ is. So we talk about Christ.

Ellen White says it well. "In Him there is joy that is not uncertain and unsatisfying. If the light that flows from Jesus has come to you, and you are reflecting it upon others, you show that you have joy that is pure, elevating, and ennobling. Why should not the religion of Christ be represented as it really is, as full of attractiveness and power? Why should we not present before the world the loveliness of Christ? Why do we not show that we have a living Savior, one who can walk with us in the darkness as well as in the light, and that we can trust in Him?"[1]

Today Adventist lifestyle isn't even that unusual anymore. Many people promote diets similar to ours. Even the U.S. surgeon general has warnings on cigarettes and alcohol. People aren't sticking their heads in the sand anymore about healthy living. While it is possible for us still to be leaders in the area of health, my own opinion is that the opportunity has largely passed. Now it is time to lead in other ways.

Though, I must say, one of the bravest acts in Adventism that I have personally witnessed took place this past summer at a reenactment and involved a lifestyle issue. Several Adventists belong to our group, so by now it's pretty common knowledge what we will and will not eat. Overall, people are very considerate and even make an effort to accommodate us when the need arises. It's not as if we're persecuted for our beliefs or anything. But one day while a bunch of us were sitting around under the fly of the cooking tent ignoring the heat, a young man who apparently wasn't yet familiar with the topic mentioned to one of the young Adventist women present not to get the lobster at a famous fast-food chain because it wasn't very good.

I would have let a remark like that pass with a chuckle and the assurance that I certainly wouldn't try the lobster; but not this brave young woman. She boldly told him that she wouldn't eat lobster anyway, and when he questioned her, she stood up for what she believed in a way that filled me with admiration. She was firm but not pushy, and he (along with everyone else present) left that conversation knowing exactly where she stood. Period.

She didn't try to convert him to a kosher diet or cajole him into being a vegetarian. Nor did she even spend needless energy worrying over what he might think of her after the conversation (even when it was pretty clear that he thought we were all off our rockers). Instead she simply stood up for what she believed in a straightforward manner and left the consequences to God. I learned quite a lot that day about courage under fire.

So I'm not saying we should never explain our beliefs—we should. And we should be prepared to defend them if necessary. But I think that we should let the Holy Spirit make the judgment call on when it's time to stand up or not. That day it wasn't my place to say anything, except to support the young woman in what she said. But I realized that she passed with flying colors, while had I been in her place I would have failed miserably. God needs bold people to share Him with the world.

One thing that we all have for sharing in abundance is joy.

JOY

My husband and I are dotty over Adventist Frontier Missions.[2] We read their magazine from cover to cover the first Sabbath after it arrives. Once, on a canoe trip, we brought the magazine with us, and we both wanted to read it. Since I'd already gone through one or two stories, I ripped them out and gave them to him. Then as I finished a story I would tear it out and pass it over. We read that magazine, literally, from cover to cover.

The refreshing thing about the magazine is that the missionaries talk about what's going on in their lives—how God is challenging them and how they are relating to the people around them, occasionally to other missionaries, but more often to the people groups they are living with. And no matter what they write about, whether it's the bugs in the flour, the disease-carrying mosquitoes, or the trouble they're having with the language, their joy beams through like a spotlight. Instead of focusing on the immediate day-to-day problems, they keep their eyes on the future. Any and every inconvenience is a fleeting thing, while what really matters is eternal.

Here is something that each of us can apply to our own lives. I tend to get very short-tempered when I'm rushed and have too much to do or when everything I am *trying* to do doesn't come together smoothly.

Recently I attempted to prepare a five-course French lunch for the kids at my son's school, where I teach French every week. I couldn't get the custard to set for my *ouefs à la neige* (eggs in the snow). Although I made two batches, they both curdled. It's not an easy process in the first place, and by the time the second batch was ruined I'd used just about every saucepan and mixing bowl in the kitchen and was just about out of ingredients.

In the end I decided to substitute fresh vanilla pudding, using a tried-and-true recipe. By the time Rachel and I left for the school with the meal, our kitchen looked as though the Pillsbury Doughboy had exploded in it. But my focusing on the fact that the situation was temporary, that my kitchen would return to normal, as would my schedule, made the entire process nearly enjoyable. I was able to keep a cheerful attitude despite the circumstances. The custard might have curdled, but my temper didn't.

"My days are swifter than a weaver's shuttle, and are spent without hope. Oh, remember that my life is a breath!" Job moaned (Job 7:6, 7, NKJV). He was right. Each day that we receive is a precious gift. Unfortunately we are hardly ever able to appreciate that gift until it is compromised. Anyone who has ever suffered from poor health will vouch for the renewed gratitude with which they greet life when they regain their health. Likewise, those who have had a close brush with death have the same feeling, only stronger. Fortunately we don't have to wait for this type of experience in order to appreciate properly the gift of life that God has given us.

Being grateful for life each day and treating it with the respect and reverence it deserves begins by our actively thanking God for it daily. None of us on this planet live and breathe by the capricious winds of fate. We are here because God wills it. He has a plan for all our lives, a mission that is unique for each of us. No one else can take our place, because every one of us is special. Here is the *basis* for our joy.

God, our Father, first created you and me and everyone else on the planet because He loves us. And because He loves us, He wants to save us. Not desiring that we share Satan's end, He's made a provision to spare us eternal separation from Him. This is the *establishment* of our joy.

Furthermore, He has created a place where we will live in happiness, peace, and joy forever. Although none of us merit it,

He gives it to us freely, withholding nothing. We will live in heaven forever because Jesus suffered, died, and rose again for us. It will be the *fulfillment* of our joy.

Jesus said, "I have come that they may have life, and that they may have it more abundantly" (John 10:10, NKJV). So each day that we live, as we move toward the fulfillment of our joy, is to be celebrated and joy-filled. Recently I read a story that had as one of its characters an Indian woman whose name in her native tongue meant "Oh, Be Joyful."

Today let your name be Oh, Be Joyful. Begin by thanking God for His daily blessing of life. Don't be surprised if you learn to appreciate it more and abuse it less. Take a moment to be grateful for life. Once you are thankful for it, sharing joy will be a natural outcome of your gratitude, and you just might find it affecting other aspects of your life as well.

What are you grateful for? Take a few moments to jot down some of your thoughts. Be specific. Don't be satisfied with listing "the weather." Go deeper. What is it about the weather that you appreciate? Rain? Lack of it? Sunshine? Gorgeous sunsets? Snow? Concretely define the various aspects of your life. It is there that you will find places to hang your gratitude, not in the shadowy generality of vague expressions. Write things that you are grateful for here:

_____

_____

_____

_____

_____

_____

As you find yourself looking for things to appreciate you'll notice that you have begun to have a running conversation with God. This is what Paul is talking about when he says, "Rejoice always, pray without ceasing, in everything give thanks; for this is the will of God in Christ Jesus for you" (1 Thess. 5:16-18, NKJV). It's that bit about "pray[ing] without ceasing" that gets people. How, they wonder, can one pray without ceasing?

We can imagine it as cultivating a "Yes, Lord?" attitude. Anyone who has children will recognize this. It's keeping one ear open for something while doing at least three other things. For example, you may be paying the bills, talking on the phone, and making out the grocery list while almost subconsciously you are also aware of where your children are and, vaguely, of what they are doing. If things become too quiet you will go and investigate. Or if they get too rowdy you'll go referee. But it's that awareness that I have in mind. It doesn't matter what else you are doing at the moment; you still sense what's going on.

We can use that awareness to listen for God's will or to note something that we are grateful for throughout our days too, regardless of how busy we become. And best of all, it's a two-way street. As we listen for God's voice we can also send our problems and our praises to Him. Even Jesus, though He was Himself God, acknowledged having this same relationship with God the Father. "I am in the Father and the Father is in me" (John 14:11).

The next time you sit down for your devotional time I want you to try a little experiment. After praying, open your Bible. It doesn't matter which book or what chapter. Just open it to whatever you happen to feel like reading and ask God to speak to you through His Word. Whenever I do this I eventually come across a verse that applies directly to me and often addresses some problem I am having in my life. Sometimes I read only a few verses before I find something. Other times it's a few chapters, but in the end one verse always seems to jump out at me.

Now, write that verse down here:

_____

_____

_____

And use this space to record what God is specifically saying to you through the passage. Do not write what you think the biblical author meant, but how the verse speaks to you directly. What is God saying to *you*?

_____

_____

_____

_____

_____

_____

I have a journal full of such passages and the messages that God had through them for me. It thrills me that God has this way of communicating to us through a Book written so long ago. Reading the Bible this way has always made me feel as if He had it composed just for me. And it has made reading the Bible seem somewhat of a treasure hunt, too. But, most important, I feel as though God is speaking directly to me in a tangible way that I can actually hear.

No doubt you'll find other ways to develop your relationship with God that I haven't even thought of. It took me a long time to discover that knowing about God and even doing what

He wants me to do is not the same thing as *knowing* Him. The turning point for me came when I read these words spoken by Jesus: "Not everyone who says to Me, 'Lord, Lord,' shall enter the kingdom of heaven, but he who does the will of My Father in heaven. Many will say to Me in that day, 'Lord, Lord, have we not prophesied in Your name, cast out demons in Your name, and done many wonders in Your name?' And then I will declare to them, 'I never knew you; depart from Me, you who practice lawlessness!'" (Matt. 7:21-23, NKJV).

Obviously these individuals believed that they knew Jesus. They thought they were doing what He wanted them to do. But He said that He didn't know them. Why? They did not have a relationship with Him. They might have known a lot about Him and done what they assumed He wanted them to do, but they didn't know Him in a personal way.

Knowing God in this way is more than knowing *about* Him. For example, people might read every one of my books and articles or surf my Web site. They might even write me a letter, send me an e-mail, or hear me speak somewhere. Others might act in the ways that I outline in my books, articles, sermons, and speeches. In fact, they might cook all the recipes in my books and eat them every day. Yet if they are not in constant contact with me personally, I will not know them. Such individuals could walk up to me on a street and introduce themselves and tell me all the things they have been doing, and I may even be impressed. But I still do not know them.

Then I thought about all the ways that we form our relationships. Relationships grown in person are perhaps superior to others. The opportunity to see the individual we are building a relationship with provides a free give-and-take of information and verbal support. We may have trips and gatherings for special occasions or even for no occasion at all. This is the kind of relationship we all look forward to having with Christ someday.

But even-long distance relationships can flourish if the people involved are committed to it. Cards, letters, phone calls, and gifts sent across the miles all demonstrate how much we care. A long-distance relationship is the only kind we can have with God right now. It's a bit of a simplistic comparison, I agree, but you get the idea. The point is, a long-distance relationship might be harder to sustain, but it shares all its components with a more close-up relationship. Both parties must make continual efforts of support and friendship. They must jointly exchange information and feelings. For a relationship to grow, both parties must be equally invested in its growth and nourishment.

The same thing holds true in our relationship with God. Gone are the grocery-list prayers, the quick trips to the prayer closet, the lifeless rendezvous at church. It is no casual relationship that God calls us to. We are entering into communion with the Creator of the universe. What an awesome privilege we have to be friends with our God! Jesus said, "No longer do I call you servants, for a servant does not know what his master is doing; but I have called you friends, for all things that I heard from My Father I have made known to you" (John 15:15, NKJV).

Take a moment to think of the bones that form the structure of your relationships. How can you apply them to your relationship with God? He wants to know you well and infuse your life with joy in Him and in the future that He has prepared for you.

Begin your mornings with a prayer like this:

"Dear Lord, I ask You to fill me with Your joy this morning. Teach me about Yourself. Speak to me as I go through this day, guiding me at every step. Help me to remember constantly that I am not living for this life alone, but in anticipation of the one that I will share with You in heaven. Give me the strength to partner with You and help me to live a life that is acceptable in Your sight. Amen."

Today I will claim this Bible promise about joy:

_____

_____

_____

[1] Ellen G. White, *That I May Know Him,* p. 142.
[2] Adventist Frontiers, P.O. Box 346, Berrien Springs, Michigan 49103. Phone: 269-473-4250.

CHAPTER 9

JOY IN ACTION

W E CAN'T HAVE JOY IN US without its affecting our lives any more than we could have cancer in us without its altering how we live. Joy starts inside, but it prompts us to action. A life led by joy will be more concerned about God's agenda than what's written in the Dayplanner. A life of joy will always give top priority to things of eternal value. While it will not deny reality, it will always hope for the best in every situation.

Joy focuses our prayers. It automatically places us in God's will, because He is controlling our lives and every decision. What He desires is what we want. So what does this look like in everyday experience? With an abstract concept like joy it can be helpful to see it in action in a given scenario so that we are better able to recognize its working (or, conversely, its absence) in our own lives. Let's take a look at some imaginary scenarios and discuss whether what we're seeing and hearing is joy in action.

Jenny wakes up late, having forgotten to set her alarm clock. She rushes to get the children off to school and her husband to work. A stay-at-home mom, she works out of her home, so as soon as everyone is out of the house she's supposed to settle down in her "office" and transcribe tapes for her clientele of physicians.

Before she can get settled in she realizes the house is a mess and starts to straighten it up. Suddenly an hour has gone by. Because she's working on a rush job, she abandons the cleaning and begins to work frantically. But she hasn't finished by the time the children come home, and their chatter irritates her as she tries to get supper on the table and figure out where to cram in the extra hours. *This is so unfair,* she thinks. *How come I have to do everything? Can't my husband take care of some of this so I can be free to get my work done? Why is it that I'm still working and my husband is playing with the kids? Am I a maid? What's going on here? I can't keep this up.*

By the time Jenny goes to bed she is seething with suppressed anger (which she believes Christians shouldn't display) and is filled with frustration because she did not accomplish all that she needed to do. When she wakes up, the unfinished emotional and physical business from the day before will create a snowball that in the end will roll right over her.

Is Jenny living in joy? (I gave you a pretty easy one to start with.) No, certainly not. I don't think anyone was stumped there. Jenny started her day out the wrong way and got caught in a vicious cycle of her own making. But she probably doesn't see it that way, because she's blaming her problems on others.

Her story isn't so far-fetched. Probably most of us have had days similar to Jenny's. I know I have. The scary part—to me—is how easy it is to fall into this particular sort of trap, this self-perpetuating destructive cycle. Not only is Jenny not living in joy, she isn't even aware that she *ought to be!*

Let's play counselor to her for a minute. First, what should Jenny be doing before anything else? Praying, of course. I'll admit that this is a hard one for me. I don't do mornings, so it's a bit more than I can manage to interact intelligently before late morning. Still, we all (even I if I force myself to admit it) have time to say a quick prayer before rolling out of bed. It doesn't have to be long, and it doesn't have to incorporate every single prayer request on your list. A simple "Lord, give me the strength to do Your will today" is better than nothing. By petitioning God's help, perhaps you'll find that you suddenly have time later for Bible study and prayer.

Jenny was also letting herself get distracted by her surroundings. Rather than setting priorities and sticking to them, she was off chasing wild geese, cleaning when she should have been working, working when she should have been taking care of her children. Solomon said, "To everything there is a season, a time for every purpose under heaven" (Eccl. 3:1, NKJV).

Her thought processes were also crowding out any chance she might have had for joy to influence her life. Did you notice that they were all negative? Such negative thoughts are straight from Satan. He loves to discourage us. The only way to stop them is to stop them. Say "No!" out loud and forcefully if you have to when you notice such thoughts entering your head. Then replace them with God-honoring thoughts. Jenny's might have run like this: *I certainly don't feel like cleaning while my husband and children play. I'll ask them to help me, and then we can all play*. Assuming they do help, it will go a long way toward dissolving her pent-up anger and frustration. And if not, she could remind herself, *My husband is a good man, and he's doing the best he can. I love him very much, and if I lost him tomorrow I would be devastated. If I was alone, I would have to do everything myself and wouldn't blame him for not doing his share. Everything I do to take care of our family is a blessing from me to them. I enjoy blessing my family with the work that I do*.

Finally, Jenny is shutting down all avenues to joy by letting anger, resentment, and frustration build in her heart instead of releasing these destructive feelings. We have feelings for a reason. They are to alert us to something in our lives. So-called negative emotions, such as anger, frustration, fear, or irritation, signal us that something is wrong. They become sins when we act on them in hurtful ways. But we can—and should—use them to prompt us to take action that will keep us from sinning. If Jenny's frustration stems from too great a workload, she should consider cutting back. If her anger is a result of feeling used and abused by her family, she should speak to them about how she feels and see if they will commit to helping her with the housework.

Let's follow Ben's day. He is an engineer with a highly aggressive personality. Every morning he rises early for a six-mile run. Then he prepares for his workday. Single, he has several pets, two of whom are increasingly senile and use the house as bathroom facilities. Ben has a rigorous Bible study schedule. Every morning before work he puts in a full hour reading the Bible and looking up and comparing texts. Then he has a brief prayer and leaves for work.

Ben's workdays are long, though he does manage to make it home for his lunch hour to let his pets out, clean up any messes, and take the dog for a short walk. A mental to-do list consumes Ben's thought processes. When he finally reaches home he's pretty tired and likes to eat his supper in front of the television. Sometimes he spends the rest of the night there, falling asleep on the couch. Other nights he might play a computer game or surf the Internet. Very rarely does he go out with friends. The next day he gets up and does it all over again.

Is Ben living a joyful life? What do you think? I'd have to say that I don't think so. His Bible study seems more like cramming for a test than building a relationship with God, but only he and God know for sure. Except for the attention he gives his pets, the rest of his life is totally self-centered. Ben might live "by the Book," but it isn't much of a life. I think God has so much more in store for us. It's like the millionaire's son living under a bridge and eating at the homeless shelter. Why would he do something like that with his father's endless resources at his disposal? We're the King's kids, and we shouldn't be living like paupers. "And my God shall supply all your need according to His riches in glory by Christ Jesus" (Phil. 4:19, NKJV).

What do you think about Noreen? Married and a career woman, she and her husband, Douglas, decided early in their marriage that their careers were important and that they wanted to pursue them for a while and postpone having a family. Noreen continues to be happy with this decision, though Douglas has recently suggested it might be time to start think- ing about a family. But as a concert pianist, Noreen would have to put her career on hold indefinitely to have children, and she doesn't feel ready for that. But she's also open to what God wants for her life. Douglas and Noreen have prayed together about this step.

At work Noreen deals with persecution from a viola player who feels inferior to her and makes her professional life difficult. Although Noreen tries to deal with the person in a kind way, the stress is getting to her and makes practicing and concerts fraught with tension and strife. She wonders if perhaps God is trying to tell her to give up her career, possibly for a family, or that her life should take another direction. *Why is this person against me?* she asks herself. *What have I done? Show me what to do, Lord. I know peace is important to You. Do You want me to leave my position in this symphony? Where do You want me to go? How can I resolve this situation?*

Because of her difficult home schedule and time-consuming

travel program Noreen struggles to find time for Bible study and prayer. Rather than sitting down for a long stretch of time, she breaks her time up. On her lunch break she takes a "prayer walk" wherever she is. During it she prays for herself, her husband, her job, and the things that concern her. Whenever she brushes her teeth she prays for people she knows. She carries her Bible and a small notebook with her wherever she goes so that any time she has to wait she can study.

Noreen is a pretty easy case. We can see how connected she is with God. She relies on Him to lead her. Even though trials and uncertainty do fill her life, she has faith that God will work things out, and she's determined that they should come out His way rather than hers or even Douglas's.

Throughout these little scenarios, have you noticed how important self-talk is? First, it acts like a thermometer. It takes our spiritual temperature pretty accurately. If I had skipped the entire story and left only the self-talk, you could easily have decided whether Jenny and Noreen were living a joyful life. The trouble with such self-talk is that it's easy to ignore. We don't give it the significance it deserves and thus make no attempt to regulate or control it. But the Bible tells us: "And do not be conformed to this world, but be transformed by the renewing of your mind, that you may prove what is that good and acceptable and perfect will of God" (Rom. 12:2, NKJV). Our minds can't be transformed if the negative thoughts that go through them don't get rooted out. We have to stop negative thoughts at their starting point. Do you recognize any of these?

I'll never get this right.

You always do that, and I hate it.

That's not fair!

This situation is hopeless—it will never change.

If only he would stop doing that, then I could change.

I hate that.

I can't stand it when she does that.

Satan invented every one of these thoughts. Listen—can you hear him?

I'll never get this right. (I'm stupid and sinful and deserve to fail. I'm not worth saving.)

You always do that, and I hate it. (You're the cause of all my problems. I hate you.)

That's not fair! (That's not fair to me, and I'm what is important in this situation.)

This situation is hopeless—it will never change. (We're doomed. No one can save us. No one is powerful enough to change anything. Not even God.)

If only he would stop doing that, then I could change. (It's your fault that I behave the way I do, and I am powerless to change unless you change first.)

I hate that. (Hate is the opposite of love.)

I can't stand it when she does that. (She's so stupid, clumsy, thoughtless, and impossible, and will never learn. No one can love her. I certainly can't love her, and neither can God.)

If we allow these types of thoughts (and many more) to run through our minds, what will happen to our attitude? And if our attitude is negative, what kind of actions will result? It may start out as just a simple thought, but in the end it will result in deeds. The types of actions you perform will be based on the types of thoughts that you cultivate.

Changing negative thought patterns is hard. We each have our own "tracks" of negative thoughts that automatically start racing through our minds when we get upset. If you pay attention, you will catch the same thoughts running again and again through your mind. Try to capture them before they get out of control. Write them here so you will begin to notice them when they pop up.

Negative thoughts I have:	*Positive thoughts to replace them:*
_____	_____
_____	_____
_____	_____
_____	_____
_____	_____

But it's not enough simply to know what they are—or even to remove them. "When an unclean spirit goes out of a man, he goes through dry places, seeking rest, and finds none. Then he says, 'I will return to my house from which I came.' And when he comes, he finds it empty, swept, and put in order. Then he goes and takes with him seven other spirits more wicked than himself, and they enter and dwell there; and the last state of that man is worse than the first. So shall it also be with this wicked generation" (Matt. 12:43-45, NKJV). We must replace negative Satan-honoring thoughts with positive God-honoring ones. For example, here is a positive replacement thought for each of the examples listed above:

I'll never get this right. ("I can do all things through Christ who strengthens me" [Phil. 4:13, NKJV]).

You always do that, and I hate it. (I do not like it when you do that, but I love you, and I can treat you with respect and love even if I don't feel like it, because the Holy Spirit is living in me.)

That's not fair! (Life is certainly not fair. But how can this situation bless someone?)

This situation is hopeless—it will never change. (Life here may be hopeless, but something far greater awaits us. I'll think about that instead of this temporary setback.)

If only he would stop doing that, then I could change. (In what ways am I causing him to act like that toward me? Is there something I could change in my behavior toward him or in my reaction to him that would help this situation? God, help me to love him despite how I feel toward him right now.)

I hate that. (I may not like this situation, but God put me here for a reason. Show me what You want me to do in this situation, Lord.)

I can't stand it when she does that. (I do not like her actions, but I love her because God loves her. And I will treat her the way God would if He were here in my place, or the way I would like to be treated if I were in her place.)

If you're thinking this is similar to the game Pollyanna played, you're right. If you look for the silver lining behind each dark cloud, what do you see? The silver lining. But if you simply look at the black clouds and scowl, what do you notice only? The black clouds. The question is Which would you rather look at?

Of course, I'm making it sound as though we have a choice in each situation, but really, as Christians trying to reach our potential in Christ, we have only one choice. If we choose Christ we also elect to allow Him to renew our minds. Our part is to catch our negative thoughts and replace them with positive ones. The Holy Spirit can quicken our conscience so that we are sensitive to such thoughts. And if you can't think of a positive thought, you can pray for one. God is more than willing to help and empower us in this process.

Years ago a friend of mine was going through a tough time. Her husband took the money they intended to place as a down payment on a house and used it for his own enjoyment. He bought drugs, hired a limo, and picked up a woman he'd just met. They flew to some obscure island. By the time he had sobered up he had bought a bar on the island and was flat broke.

I don't recall how they ever managed to get back.

My friend had two small children to support, and because of the experience suffered a depression so great that she said that some mornings she didn't even have the energy to lift her toothbrush. But this courageous woman taught me so much about living in joy. Whenever I started to commiserate with her she'd hold up her hands and say, "Please don't feed my 'poor me's.'" Even though she had legitimate reasons to bemoan cruel fate, she was determined not to wallow in self-pity. She was—and still is—an inspiration to me.

Becoming a joy-filled Christian doesn't happen overnight, but the rewards are eternal. You'll find that in time you'll look at life with a whole new perspective. Seeing with the eyes of Christ, you'll notice things you never saw before. The Holy Spirit will prompt you to act in ways that will bless others. Best of all, your relationship with God will flourish, because you will be full of joy.

CHAPTER 10

I WILL JOY

S O FAR WE HAVE DISCUSSED WAYS in which joy will change our choices, our actions, and our perspective. But joy can affect us in still another way. Proverbs tells us that "a joyful heart is good medicine, but a broken spirit dries up the bones" (Prov. 17:22, NASB). A lack of joy can make us physically ill, while its presence helps us like a "good medicine." Joy is a heavenly prescription for health!

We've all heard about or read the latest medical advice that says turning your anger inward and suppressing your feelings can make you sick. Or the stories about seriously ill people who made themselves laugh by watching funny movies and in the process became well. What's inside us, emotionally speaking, can hurt us or help us. A recent article in the health magazine *Vibrant Life* states that "a growing number of health experts believe that depression affects the body to such an extent that it causes irregular heart rhythms or the progression of arteriosclerosis (hardening and/or thickening of the arteries), which blocks the blood's flow. Others suggest that depression might adversely affect motivation, and people stop doing the things that keep their hearts healthy, says Robert Carney."[1]

I WILL JOY

The article goes on to report that "James Fauerbach, Ph.D., of Johns Hopkins, says that although we're only beginning to understand how to foster positive outlooks, research from a wide array of sources suggests that certain behaviors may be beneficial, starting with an old cliché to which he's added some words of wisdom: 'Those who see the glass as half empty and who take on life from a defensive posture are likely to experience more negative effects than those who see the glass as half full and who seek to make the most of their present circumstances.'"[2]

How we act and react in life is important not only to those we are witnessing to, but for our own health too. Joy dictates what happens to these positive or negative feelings. When we are full of God's Spirit and living His way, He will help us process our feelings and our reaction to them. He will show us how to become proactive rather than reactive when life buffets us. "The life in which the fear of the Lord is cherished will not be a life of sadness and gloom. It is the absence of Christ that makes the countenance sad and the life a pilgrimage of sighs. . . . But Christ dwelling in the soul is a wellspring of joy. For all who receive Him, the keynote of the Word of God is 'rejoicing.'"[3]

"Today is the day that the Lord has made. Let us rejoice and be glad in it" (see Ps. 118:24). In this day. Not tomorrow, when the bills are paid. Not next month, after surgery. Not next year, when we move to a new house. Today is the day. Rejoice today no matter what today looks like.

"If Jesus had not died our sacrifice and risen again, we should never have known peace, never have felt joy, but only experienced the horrors of darkness and the miseries of despair. Then let only praise and gratitude be the language of our hearts. All our lives we have been partakers of His heavenly benefits, recipients of the blessings of His priceless atonement. Therefore it is impossible for us to conceive the low and helpless state . . . from which Christ has raised us. When we feel the pains, the sorrows and bereavements to which we are subject, let not one murmuring thought dishonor our Redeemer. . . . We cannot determine how much less we suffer than our sins deserve."[4]

It's no secret that light always looks brighter next to darkness. Some of the world's greatest painters make use of this technique. In our generation Thomas Kinkade, aptly called the "Painter of Light," has presented light against the dark to great effect. In our lives, it is true of joy. It will always be more visible against the dark canvas of suffering. One of the English officers imprisoned at Flossenbürg with Dietrich Bonhoeffer said of him, "Bonhoeffer always seemed to me to spread an atmosphere of happiness and joy over the least incident and profound gratitude for the mere fact that he was alive."

I can't help wondering about people such as Bonhoeffer who lived during such perilous times as World War II. And not simply lived but, as this man said of Bonhoeffer, "spread an atmosphere of happiness and joy over the least incident." Our own generation is seeing the deterioration of whatever tentative type of peace has existed in our world. Stress and anxiety about the future are commonplace and far-reaching. If people of any time could use a message of joy and hope, it is we who are living in the shadow of such uncertainty and prospective disaster.

It seems to me, then, no coincidence that the list of the fruit of the Spirit has joy second (love appears first). "The fruit of the Spirit is love, joy, peace, longsuffering, kindness, goodness, faithfulness, gentleness, self-control" (Gal. 5:22, 23, NKJV). From a heart filled with love, joy will flow. All these will be ripe for the picking in the life of a Christian no matter what happens in the world around us.

Joy is a gift, and like any other gift it can be abused or neglected and lost. We can guard our joy by making sure that we nurture it constantly in the disciplines of praise, prayer, obedience, etc. Always we must protect it from people who will try to take it from us, whether they be non-Christian or Christian. Just because someone claims to be acting from a Christian motive does not mean they are. Jesus said that we are to be as wise as serpents and harmless as doves. A harmless dove will not try to steal your joy, and a wise serpent will know a harmless dove from a predatory eagle. "Test everything. Hold on to the good. Avoid every kind of evil" (1 Thess. 5:21, 22).

The one question I used to be afraid that someone would ask me was "What's so great about being a Christian?"

Christians don't suffer less than anyone else. In fact, they may suffer more. Being a Christian doesn't save you from the everyday ups and downs of life. Christianity doesn't even prevent terrible things from happening to you. On a very subconscious level, of course, I knew that our relationship with God is what helps us to get through it all, but how could you ever describe what that is like to someone who has no concept of it? After all, it is a relationship with Someone that you can't see, hear, or reach out and touch.

But I'm not afraid of that question anymore. What's so great about being a Christian? Joy. Joy is what's great about being a Christian. It makes the whole difference between the life of a Christian and someone who hasn't discovered the love of Christ yet—of walking in the light or walking in the darkness. Think of all the people in the world who are missing out on this joy because we haven't shared our good news with them. Ignorant of this holy capacity to shed the world's trouble like water off a duck's back, they can't conceive of this straining to hear, see, and experience what we know awaits us. And in the straining, if we catch a little of the wonder of heaven that colors our present world, they would not understand that, either.

Perhaps we do view the world through rose-colored glasses, in a sense, but what better way is there to see it? Joy is a much bigger gift than we have the capacity to receive. Let your joy overflow into the world around you. Color your world with joy so that everyone you meet each day of your life will notice and ask, "What's so great about being a Christian? What do you have that I don't have?"

And you can answer, "I have Jesus, and He gives me joy. He'll give it to you, too."

Then Jesus will say with John, "It gave me great joy to have some brothers come and tell about your faithfulness to the truth and how you continue to walk in the truth. I have no greater joy than to hear that my children are walking in the truth" (3 John 3, 4).

Walk in the truth. Leap in the truth. Love in the truth. Joy in the truth. And you too will have no greater joy.

---

[1] Robert Carney, as quoted in Rita Robinson, "Don't Worry; Be Happy," *Vibrant Life,* September/October 2002, p. 11.

[2] *Ibid.*

[3] Ellen G. White, *That I May Know Him,* p. 142.

[4] White, *In Heavenly Places* (Washington, D.C.: Review and Herald Pub. Assn., 1967), p. 36.